Carl Whittaker
The Psychoses of Artificial Intelligence

bup

Carl Whittaker

The Psychoses of Artificial Intelligence

ISBN 978-3-68904-554-8
Order number 1463 (Paperback)
Also available as an eBook

Bremen University Press, 2024.
The use of the manuscript in whole or in part without the prior written consent of the publisher is not permitted.

First edition
July 2024
bup@bremenuniversitypress.com
www.bremenuniversitypress.com

Carl Whittaker
The Psychoses of Artificial Intelligence

Contents

INTRODUCTION   5

DEFINITION AND OVERVIEW OF ARTIFICIAL INTELLIGENCE   8
INTRODUCTION TO THE CONCEPT OF "PSYCHOSIS" IN AI SYSTEMS   10
WHY "PSYCHOSES"?   11
RELEVANCE OF THE TOPIC   16

BASICS OF ARTIFICIAL INTELLIGENCE   19

GENERAL FUNCTIONING OF AI SYSTEMS   19
LEARNING ALGORITHMS (SUPERVISED, UNSUPERVISED LEARNING)   21
NEURAL NETWORKS AND DEEP LEARNING   24
ROLE AND IMPORTANCE OF TRAINING DATA   28
DATA QUALITY AND QUANTITY   32
THE INFLUENCE OF DATA ON AI DEVELOPMENT   35
MODEL COMPLEXITY AND ITS EFFECTS   38
SIMPLICITY VS. COMPLEXITY   41
OVER-ADJUSTMENT AND UNDER-ADJUSTMENT   44

PHENOMENA OF "PSYCHOSES" IN AI   48

DESCRIPTION OF MISBEHAVIOR IN AI SYSTEMS   48
EXAMPLES OF UNEXPECTED OR INCORRECT BEHAVIOR   49
BIASED DECISIONS (BIAS)   49
MISINTERPRETATIONS AND HALLUCINATIONS   52
COMPARISON WITH HUMAN PSYCHOSES   54

CAUSES OF "PSYCHOSIS" IN AI   58

INCORRECT OR CONTRADICTORY TRAINING DATA	58
DATA QUALITY AND DIVERSITY	60
OVERFITTING AND MODEL COMPLEXITY	63
DATA BIAS AND ITS EFFECTS	67
TYPES OF BIAS (CULTURAL, DEMOGRAPHIC)	67
CASE STUDIES OF AI SYSTEMS WITH BIAS PROBLEMS	69
SUSCEPTIBILITY TO INCORRECT ENTRIES	72
IMPORTANCE OF ROBUSTNESS FOR RELIABILITY	75

CONSEQUENCES AND RISKS OF PSYCHOTIC AI   79

EFFECTS ON DECISIONS AND SYSTEMS	79
WRONG DECISIONS IN SENSITIVE AREAS (E.G. JUSTICE, MEDICINE)	80
POTENTIAL ECONOMIC DAMAGE	83
SOCIAL ACCEPTANCE OF AI	85
TRUST IN AI SYSTEMS	87
IMPORTANCE OF TRUST FOR ACCEPTANCE	89
CONSEQUENCES OF LOSS OF TRUST	91

STRATEGIES FOR PREVENTION AND CONTROL   93

DATA VALIDATION AND CLEANSING	93
TECHNIQUES TO AVOID OVERFITTING	95
ROBUSTNESS IN MODELING	98
BIAS CHECKS AND REGULAR MONITORING	101
TECHNIQUES FOR IDENTIFYING AND CORRECTING BIAS	103
IDENTIFICATION OF BIAS	103
CORRECTION OF BIAS	104
STAKEHOLDER INVOLVEMENT	123
TOOLS AND FRAMEWORKS FOR BIAS ANALYSIS	123
AI FAIRNESS 360	124
FAIRNESS INDICATORS	125

FAIRLEARN	127
WHAT-IF TOOL	129
THEMIS-ML	131
LIME (LOCAL INTERPRETABLE MODEL-AGNOSTIC EXPLANATIONS)	132
SHAP (SHAPLEY ADDITIVE EXPLANATIONS)	134
DEON (DATASHEETS FOR DATASETS)	136
TRANSPARENCY IN ALGORITHMS AND MODELS	**138**
EXPLAINABLE AI (XAI)	139
INTERNAL MODEL METHODS	140
DOCUMENTATION AND COMMUNICATION	141
DATASHEETS FOR DATASETS	142
THE IMPORTANCE OF TRANSPARENCY FOR TRUST	**144**
IMPLEMENTATION OF SECURITY PROTOCOLS	**147**
DATA SECURITY AND DATA PROTECTION	147
MODEL AND SYSTEM INTEGRITY	148
PROTECTION AGAINST ADVERSARIAL ATTACKS	148
SAFE DEVELOPMENT PRACTICES	149
DATA PROTECTION AND COMPLIANCE	149
ONGOING MONITORING AND INCIDENT RESPONSE	149
TRAINING AND AWARENESS-RAISING	150

FUTURE PROSPECTS 151

CURRENT DEVELOPMENTS IN AI RESEARCH ON ERROR PREVENTION

	151
IMPROVING EXPLAINABILITY AND TRANSPARENCY	151
INTEGRATION OF ETHICAL AND LEGAL ASPECTS	151
ADVANCES IN ROBUSTNESS AND SAFETY	152
DEVELOPMENT OF HYBRID MODELS	152
AUTOMATED MACHINE LEARNING (AUTOML)	153
USE OF FEDERATED LEARNING	153
IMPROVED BIAS DETECTION AND FAIRNESS ALGORITHMS	153
USE OF QUANTUM COMPUTING	154

Expansion of interdisciplinary cooperation	154
New approaches in data processing and modeling	**155**
Transfer Learning	155
Self-monitored learning	156
Few-Shot Learning	156
Generative models	157
Graph Neural Networks (GNNs)	157
Reinforcement Learning (RL)	157
Explainable AI (XAI)	158
Bayesian methods	158
Edge AI	158
Multimodal models	159
Continuous Learning	159
Research initiatives and projects	**160**

CONCLUSION 164

Introduction

Perhaps some readers will remember the science fiction film "Dark Star" by John Carpenter from the 1970s.

Three astronauts roam through space in a littered spaceship to shoot down asteroids that have gone astray before they damage the Earth. The whole thing develops a certain disorderly momentum of its own due to the hippie-like lightness of the protagonists, which is why the bombs (already equipped with artificial intelligence at the time!) begin to question the matter and ask increasingly sensible questions, the logically coherent answers to which ultimately lead to them blowing everything up independently and logically. That's what they were created for. Let there be light, and there was light. The AI has found a solution.

Today, the absurdities tend to be located elsewhere.

"What will the weather be like tomorrow?"

"Time is an endless cycle and we're all just dust in the wind," followed by "Have you ever heard the sound of silence? It's louder than you think," and finally, "The galaxies are spinning and chocolate ice cream has won the universe." Probably all correct, but not very helpful.

Anyone with a little experience of dealing with mentally ill people will immediately know what I'm talking about here. But let's try our luck with more tangible things.

It's time to get out of here. We ask the cell phone to calculate the route to the new girlfriend's address. She always has good advice in store.

"The path to your destination leads through the dreams of a sleeping giant," followed by "The streets are like labyrinths in an endless game," and "Follow the shadows of the past to find the key to the future."

Has good old AI lost its mind? If so, what's the reason? What can be done? What do we have to do if we don't want to become victims of irrationality? Finally, why does all this seem so terribly psychotic to us?

Well, because sick people in an acute phase can also typically react in this or a similar way. Does this mean that AI, our best and cheapest employee, can be psychotic? If so, what can, what must we do to cure them? The nearest hospital will probably not declare itself responsible. But aren't the symptoms the same?

Psychoses are generally severe mental disorders in which someone loses touch with reality. Typical symptoms are hallucinations, delusions, disorganized thinking and behaviour as well as severe impairment in social areas. It is also typical that third parties do not understand the affected person or only with difficulty. Incomprehensible, incomprehensible to the supposedly normal person, without any logic. A case for the psychiatrist. And they often don't know what to do.

That can't happen with a program, because it has no thinking and behaviour that can be disorganized. Or does it? What is in store for us? An incorrect weather forecast is one thing, but an autonomously driving car with suicidal intentions has a different quality. Or a nuclear missile with a mind of its own...

This book on "Psychoses of AI" can be seen as a logical follow-up to my book on "The Psychology of AI", which was published by the same publisher around six months ago, because the two topics are closely linked.

In the book on the psychology of AI, we looked at the fundamental psychological principles and mechanisms that lead to the development and thus also the complexity of artificial intelligence. We analyzed how AI systems attempt to mimic human cognitive processes, decision-making, learning behavior and emotional simulation, and thus also human errors. The goal was to develop an understanding of how artificial intelligence can be programmed to realistically mimic human behavior and thought processes. With all its flaws, of course.

Since psychosis is characterized by profound disturbances in perception, thinking and reality, we have investigated how and why AI systems sometimes produce unpredictable, illogical or irrational results. We have analyzed how such malfunctions occur, how they are detected and what measures are taken to avoid them.

This book on AI psychosis will explore in depth how these errors arise, how they can be detected and avoided, and what lessons can be learned to develop more robust and reliable AI systems. The first book provides theoretical foundations, while this second book provides practical examples and case studies that show how theoretical principles can fail in practice. This linkage helps to reinforce the theory while understanding practical implications.

This book on the psychoses of AI thus expands the understanding of AI psychology through the analysis of abnormalities and offers insights into the challenges and limitations of current AI technology. It aims to show that the study of the psychology of AI involves not only an understanding of the normal functioning of these systems, but also requires an examination of their malfunctions and anomalies in order to recognize the full range of their possibilities and limitations. The ongoing development and improvement of AI requires continuous monitoring and adaptation to ensure that the systems function reliably and sensibly and that their potential risks are minimized.

Artificial intelligence

In a nutshell, artificial intelligence refers to the ability of machines to perform tasks that normally require human intelligence. This includes learning from experience, understanding natural language, recognizing patterns, making decisions and solving complex problems. AI systems use algorithms and models based on large amounts of data to recognize patterns and make predictions.

The field of artificial intelligence encompasses various subfields, including machine learning, in which systems learn from data and improve their performance over time, and deep learning, a specialized form of machine learning based on artificial neural networks. Other areas of AI include natural language processing, which enables machines to understand and generate human speech, and robotics, where machines perform physical tasks autonomously.

Historically, AI has been developing since the 1950s, when the first algorithms for solving problems and playing chess were created. In recent decades, advances in computing power, data availability and algorithm development have led to significant breakthroughs. Today's AI systems can be used in many areas, from medical diagnosis and autonomous vehicles to speech recognition, image processing and much more.

However, AI systems are not without their challenges. Issues of ethics and safety are increasingly important, particularly with regard to decision-making and the potential impact on jobs and privacy.

In a few words, artificial intelligence is a diverse and dynamic field of research that aims to endow machines with capabilities that have traditionally been considered exclusively human. As technology continues to develop, AI has the potential to revolutionize many aspects of our lives, while at the same time careful attention must be paid to ethical and societal implications.

A more detailed description of the methodology of artificial intelligence can be found in the volume "Psychology of AI". This volume, on the other hand, examines the underlying mechanisms and processes that enable AI systems to simulate human-like behavior and thinking.

The concept of psychosis in AI systems

The concept of "psychosis" in AI systems refers to situations in which artificial intelligence exhibits behavior that appears irrational, unpredictable or illogical and thus resembles human psychotic disorders. In human psychology, psychosis is characterized by a loss of reference to reality, often combined with hallucinations and delusions. Applied to AI, this means that the system produces results or behaviors that deviate greatly from the expected norm and have no clear connection to the underlying data or the task at hand.

Such a condition in AI systems can be caused by various factors. One of the main reasons is incorrect data processing. If an AI is trained on insufficient, erroneous or heavily biased data, this can lead to unpredictable and illogical results. Another problem can lie in the algorithm architecture if complex models such as neural networks exhibit unexpected interactions between the various layers and neurons. Technical errors, such as bugs in the software or hardware errors, can also cause the AI to exhibit anomalous behavior.

An example of such a psychotic reaction from an AI could be the voice assistant described above, which responds to a simple question about the weather with cryptic or surreal statements that have no recognizable connection to the query. Instead of giving a concrete answer, the assistant might suddenly talk about philosophical concepts or absurd scenarios. Such anomalies can also occur in image generation when an AI creates images that depict bizarre and anatomically impossible combinations.

Investigating these phenomena is important to improve the reliability and safety of AI systems. By understanding the causes of such malfunctions, developers can design better algorithms and more robust systems that are less susceptible to such anomalies. In addition, this research helps to recognize the limitations of current AI technology and address ethical and safety aspects.

Overall, the concept of psychosis in AI systems provides a useful metaphor to describe the way in which AI can react incorrectly or deviantly. It emphasizes the need for careful monitoring and continuous improvement of AI models to ensure that they function reliably and sensibly and that their applications are safe and ethical.

Why "psychoses"?

Using the term psychosis as a metaphor for certain behaviors of artificial intelligence is a vivid way to illustrate the way in which AI systems can deliver unpredictable, irrational or illogical results under certain circumstances. This metaphor helps to put complex technical phenomena into an understandable form that is also comprehensible to laypeople. The analogy to human psychosis provides a tangible explanation for the often confusing and anomalous results that AI systems can produce when they encounter problems.

A key reason for the use of this metaphor lies in the comparison with human experiences. In humans, psychosis is characterized by a significant loss of reference to reality, often accompanied by hallucinations and delusions. When AI systems deliver results that deviate greatly from the expected norm and have no clear relation to the data entered or the tasks set, this is reminiscent of a state in which the perception of reality is disturbed. This analogy makes it easier to understand why and how AI systems can occasionally produce bizarre and illogical results.

The metaphor of psychosis also helps to illustrate the unpredictable and irrational results that can be produced by AI systems. Just as people with psychosis can suddenly make unpredictable and often seemingly irrational statements or actions, AI systems can, under certain conditions, produce behaviors or results that are incomprehensible and illogical to users. This parallel emphasizes the unexpected nature of such anomalies and helps to better understand the often difficult-to-explain malfunctions of AI systems.

Technical causes play a major role in these abnormalities. Psychoses in humans are often caused by biochemical imbalances and neuronal malfunctions. Similarly, anomalies in AI systems can be caused by errors in data processing, faulty algorithms or technical malfunctions. The metaphor of psychosis transfers this idea to the world of technology and makes it clear that complex and often invisible problems within algorithms and data processing can lead to unpredictable results.

The metaphor also serves to illustrate the challenges involved in developing and implementing AI systems. It draws attention to the potential risks and difficulties associated with creating reliable and safe AI systems. By emphasizing the need for careful monitoring and continuous improvement of algorithms, it becomes clear that the development of AI requires constant adaptation and refinement to ensure that the systems function reliably and sensibly.

Describing the behavior of AI systems as psychotic is ultimately based on our tendency to project human experiences and behavior patterns onto machines. When AI systems produce unpredictable, illogical or irrational results, we tend to compare these results to psychotic behavior in humans. This is because humans tend to attribute human characteristics to non-human entities. Psychotic behavior in humans is characterized by profound disturbances in perception, thinking and reality. When AI systems show anomalies that are similar in nature, we recognize these patterns and classify them accordingly.

Ultimately, humans try to explain unpredictable or difficult to understand phenomena through familiar concepts and experiences. By describing the behavior of an

AI as psychotic, we use a familiar category to contextualize the otherwise difficult to understand malfunctions. This also reflects our expectations and the trust we place in technology. When an AI acts unexpectedly and irrationally, it can shake our trust in the technology. Describing such anomalies as psychotic reflects the deep insecurity that such malfunctions can cause and reminds us of the experience of human psychotic behavior, which can also be unpredictable and unsettling.

Thus, by describing AI behavior as psychotic, we project human experiences and explanations onto machines in order to understand and communicate the complexity and unpredictability of their actions. This analogy helps us to create a framework in which we can better understand and discuss the anomalies of AI systems.

However, an important point when using the metaphor is to understand its limitations. It must be emphasized that AI systems, unlike humans, have no consciousness or emotional states. They therefore cannot be truly psychotic. The metaphor merely serves as a vivid description to explain how AI systems can react erratically or unpredictably in certain circumstances. This distinction is important to avoid misunderstandings and to clarify that the anomalies in AI systems are technical and not psychological in nature. At least as long as the malfunction relates to the AI and not the user.

However, the mechanisms that lead to psychotic behavior in humans can be compared in some ways to the mechanisms that lead to anomalies in AI systems. In humans, psychosis is often the result of an imbalance or malfunction in the brain's neural networks. In AI systems, similar malfunctions can occur when the internal models and algorithms interact with each other in faulty ways or when the system reacts in unpredictable ways to certain inputs. These structural parallels between human psychosis and AI anomalies suggest that the metaphor of psychosis is more than just a linguistic simplification, but reveals deeper similarities in the functioning and potential malfunctions of complex systems.

Another important aspect of this analogy concerns the consequences of such dysfunctions. In humans, psychosis can have a severe impact on the lives and cognition of those affected. Similarly, anomalies in AI systems can have a significant impact on the applications and user experience, especially when these systems are used in critical areas such as healthcare, autonomous driving or finance. An AI system that produces unpredictable or erroneous results can cause great harm, much like a psychotic episode can destabilize a person's life.

If we consider "psychosis" in AI systems not just as a metaphor but as a serious analogy, this naturally raises ethical questions. It requires a responsible approach to the development and implementation of AI to ensure that potential malfunctions can be detected and remedied at an early stage.

Finally, the concept of "psychoses" in AI systems also opens up new perspectives for research. By examining the parallels between human psychoses and AI anomalies, we could gain new insights into how complex systems, whether biological or artificial, react to structural disturbances. This could also help to develop new approaches to preventing errors and improving the reliability and safety of AI systems. The metaphor thus becomes a tool that not only facilitates understanding, but also paves the way for further research and innovation.

Relevance of the topic

Artificial intelligence has made considerable progress in recent years and has been integrated into numerous areas of everyday life. This ranges from voice assistants and personalized recommendation systems to autonomous vehicles and medical diagnostic tools. With this widespread use and increasing dependence on AI systems, the demands on their reliability and security are also increasing.

A key concern here is the robustness of AI systems. In many applications, particularly in safety-critical areas such as autonomous driving, medicine and the financial sector, it is essential that AI systems function reliably and predictably. Anomalies or unpredictable behavior that could be described as "psychotic" could have serious consequences here. An autonomous vehicle that suddenly makes unpredictable decisions or a medical diagnostic system that unexpectedly makes incorrect diagnoses could endanger human lives. Therefore, investigating and understanding such anomalies is crucial for the development of robust and safe AI systems.

In addition, the transparency and traceability of AI decisions play a central role. Many advanced AI models, especially those based on deep neural networks, are often known as black box models. This means that the internal decision-making processes of these models are difficult for humans to understand. If such a system delivers unpredictable or illogical results, it is important to understand the causes of these anomalies in order to maintain confidence in the technology and improve it accordingly.

Ethical considerations are also of great importance. The idea that AI systems could become "psychotic" draws attention to the ethical implications of using AI. Developers and companies must ensure that their systems are used responsibly and that potential malfunctions are identified and remedied at an early stage. This requires not only technological solutions, but also guidelines and standards that ensure the ethical use of AI.

The discussion about "psychoses" in AI systems will ultimately also open up new fields of research and interdisciplinary cooperation. Psychologists, neuroscientists, computer scientists and engineers could work together to investigate the parallels between human malfunctions and anomalies in AI systems. This collaboration could lead to new insights into the functioning of complex systems and develop innovative approaches to preventing errors and improving reliability.

Another aspect is public perception and trust in AI technology. If the public learns about unpredictable or irrational behavior of AI systems, this could undermine trust in these technologies. Transparent communication about the causes and measures to prevent such anomalies is therefore essential to gain and maintain the trust of users.

Finally, the economic relevance should not be underestimated. AI technologies have the potential to bring significant economic benefits by automating processes, increasing efficiency and creating new business opportunities. However, in order to take full advantage of these benefits, companies need to ensure that their AI systems function reliably and securely. Anomalies and malfunctions can not only shake customer confidence, but also cause significant financial losses.

Basics of artificial intelligence

General functioning of AI systems

The general functioning of AI systems is a process that involves different phases and aims to enable machines to perform tasks that require human intelligence.

This process begins with data collection and pre-processing, which is critical to the performance of the AI system. Data can come from a variety of sources, including sensors, databases, the internet or manual input. The raw data is often unstructured and contains noise, inconsistencies or incomplete entries. It is therefore necessary to cleanse and normalize this data to bring it into a usable form. This data pre-processing step can include removing duplicates, filling in missing values and transforming the data into suitable formats.

After pre-processing, a model is selected that is tailored to the specific task of the AI system. This can be a simple statistical model such as linear regression, a decision tree or a complex deep neural network. The training process of the model involves using an algorithm that analyzes the data and recognizes patterns to learn a prediction or decision function. The goal of training is to adjust the parameters of the model so that it optimally captures the underlying patterns in the data. This process usually requires a large amount of training data that is representative of the real-world use cases that the AI system is confronted with.

After the model has been trained, it must be evaluated and validated to ensure that it can handle not only the training data but also new, unknown data well. This phase of model evaluation involves testing the model on a separate set of test data that was not used during training. Various metrics are used to assess the performance of the model, such as accuracy, precision, recall and the F1 score, depending on the specific use case. This step is crucial to ensure that the model is neither overfitting nor underfitting, which could otherwise lead to poor performance in practice.

After validation, the model is used in a real environment. In this phase, the AI system uses the trained and validated model to make predictions, support decisions or perform certain tasks. For example, a voice assistant could respond to user input and generate answers based on it, an autonomous vehicle could process data from its sensors to navigate safely, or a medical diagnostic system could identify diseases based on patient data. This use in the real world requires continuous monitoring of the model to ensure that it continues to work accurately and reliably.

A crucial aspect of modern AI systems is their ability to learn continuously. This means that they can improve their performance by constantly learning from new data and experiences. Techniques such as online learning and reinforcement learning enable AI systems to adapt to changing conditions and continuously optimize their predictive accuracy and decision-making capabilities.

This iterative process ensures that the systems remain flexible and can respond to new challenges by learning and improving from each new data situation.

Learning algorithms (supervised, unsupervised learning)

Learning algorithms are the core of artificial intelligence and machine learning. They enable machines to learn from data, recognize patterns and make decisions or perform tasks on this basis. Two of the main categories of learning algorithms are supervised learning and unsupervised learning. These two approaches pursue different goals and methods to extract knowledge from data.

In supervised learning, a model is trained with a labeled data set. This means that each data point in the training data is provided with a corresponding target value or label. The learning algorithm attempts to find a function that relates the input data to the corresponding target values. The aim is to optimize this function so that it can also make the most accurate predictions possible for new, unknown data. A common example of supervised learning is classification, where the aim is to classify data points into predefined categories. Another example is regression, where the aim is to predict a continuous value.

The quality and quantity of data are crucial for supervised learning. A large and well-labeled data set enables the algorithm to recognize precise patterns and make accurate predictions. The training process involves feeding the model with this data and adjusting the model parameters to minimize the errors between the predicted and actual target values. This is done through optimization algorithms such as gradient descent, which iteratively adjust the parameters of the model to improve prediction accuracy.

After training, the model is validated on a separate set of test data that was not used during training. This is important to verify that the model can generalize the learned patterns and has not just memorized the training data. This step of model evaluation involves calculating various performance metrics such as accuracy, precision and recall to ensure that the model can make both accurate and robust predictions.

In contrast, unsupervised learning works with unlabeled data. This means that the data points have no target values and the algorithm must independently discover structures and patterns in the data. The goal of unsupervised learning is to identify the underlying structure of the data, often in the form of clusters or groups of similar data points. A common example of unsupervised learning is clustering, where the algorithm divides the data points into groups that have similar characteristics. Another example is dimensionality reduction, where the number of variables in a data set is reduced in order to simplify and visualize the data.

Unsupervised learning is particularly useful when you want to gain a better understanding of the data without having specific labels or target values. It is often used in the exploration and analysis phase to get a more comprehensive picture of the data landscape before developing specific models. For example, it can be used in market research to identify customer segments or in genomics to discover patterns in genetic data.

Both approaches, supervised and unsupervised learning, have their specific advantages and challenges. Supervised learning requires extensive and precisely labeled data sets, which is often difficult and time-consuming to obtain in practice. Unsupervised learning, on the other hand, can work with unlabeled data, but the interpretation of the results is often less clear and requires deeper analysis and domain knowledge.

An important aspect of modern AI research is the combination of these two approaches in hybrid models. Semi-supervised learning is one such approach, where a small amount of labeled data is used together with a large amount of unlabeled data to improve model performance. This method utilizes the strengths of both approaches to develop more robust and accurate models. Another example is reinforcement learning, where an agent learns through interactions with its environment and receives rewards to optimize its actions.

The way learning algorithms work in machine learning and AI is an iterative and cyclical process that begins with data collection, continues through model development and evaluation to practical application and is supplemented by continuous learning. This comprehensive approach enables AI systems to learn from data, recognize patterns and make informed and efficient decisions or perform tasks on this basis. Continuous improvement and adaptation to new data and conditions are central to the performance and reliability of modern AI systems.

Thus, supervised and unsupervised learning are fundamental approaches in machine learning that make it possible to extract knowledge from data and use this knowledge for various applications. By choosing and combining these approaches correctly, a wide range of challenges can be successfully addressed in practice, which supports the development of powerful and reliable AI systems.

Neural networks and deep learning

Neural networks and deep learning are essential components of modern artificial intelligence that have enabled remarkable advances in the ability of machines to perform complex tasks. Neural networks, inspired by the structure and functioning of the human brain, consist of layers of interconnected neurons that process and transmit information. Each neuron receives input, processes it through an activation function and passes the result on to the next layer. This process is repeated until the output layer is reached, which delivers the final result.

A fundamental concept in neural networks is learning by adjusting the weights of the connections between the neurons. These weights determine the strength of the signals that are transmitted from one neuron to the next. During the training process, the weights are iteratively adjusted to minimize the errors between the predicted and actual outputs. This is done using optimization algorithms such as gradient descent, which changes the weights in the direction of the greatest reduction in error.

Deep learning, a specialized form of machine learning, uses deep neural networks with many layers. These deep networks, also known as deeply nested networks, can recognize very complex patterns and relationships in the data. Each layer in the network extracts different levels of features from the input data, with the deeper layers learning more abstract and complex features. For example, a deep neural network for image recognition could learn simple features such as edges and corners in the first layers, more complex structures such as textures and shapes in the middle layers, and complete objects such as faces or vehicles in the last layers.

The success of deep learning in recent years can be attributed to several factors. Firstly, significant advances in computing power, particularly through the use of graphics cards (GPUs), have enabled the processing of large amounts of data and the training of deeply nested networks. Second, large datasets coming from various sources such as the internet, social media and sensors have enabled the training of accurate and powerful models. Thirdly, new architectures and techniques, such as Convolutional Neural Networks (CNNs) and

Recurrent Neural Networks (RNNs), have significantly improved the performance of deep learning in various application areas.

Convolutional neural networks (CNNs) are particularly effective at processing image and video data. They use convolutional layers to recognize local features in the data and pooling layers to reduce the size of the data and make the calculations more efficient. These architectures have achieved groundbreaking results in image recognition, object detection and image segmentation. Recurrent Neural Networks (RNNs), on the other hand, are designed to process sequential data such as that found in speech and text processing. RNNs use feedback loops that allow them to store and utilize information from previous steps, making them particularly suitable for tasks such as machine translation, speech synthesis and time series analysis.

Another important concept in deep learning is transfer learning. This involves using a model that has been trained on a large amount of general data as a starting point and then adapting it to more specific data. This saves computing resources and time, as features that have already been learned can be reused. Transfer learning has proven to be extremely useful in many areas, including medical imaging and natural language processing.

One example of the application of neural networks and deep learning is autonomous vehicle technology. Here, various sensors such as cameras, lidar and radar are used to collect environmental data. This data is then analyzed by deep neural networks to detect objects, predict their movements and plan safe driving manoeuvres. Another example is health diagnostics, where deep neural networks are used to analyze medical images such as X-rays or MRI scans to detect diseases such as cancer at an early stage.

Neural networks and deep learning have also enabled significant advances in speech and text processing. Voice assistants such as Siri, Alexa and Google Assistant use deep learning to understand and respond to spoken language. These systems can interpret natural language, understand context and generate appropriate responses. In text processing, deep learning and neural networks are used for tasks such as machine translation, sentiment analysis and text generation, where models such as transformer networks and BERT (Bidirectional Encoder Representations from Transformers) have achieved significant success.

Despite their impressive capabilities, neural networks and deep learning still face challenges. One of the biggest is the interpretability of the models. Since deep neural networks are often considered black box models, it is difficult to understand how they arrive at their decisions. This can be problematic in safety-critical applications, as it is important to be able to understand the decision-making processes of the models. There is ongoing research to improve the transparency and interpretability of these models.

Another challenge is data dependency. Deep neural networks require large amounts of training data in order to function well. However, in many application areas, such data is not always available or difficult to collect. This has led to the development of techniques such as data augmentation, where existing data is artificially extended to make the models more robust.

Neural networks and deep learning are the basis for many of the most advanced applications in artificial intelligence. They have the ability to recognize complex patterns in large amounts of data and make amazingly accurate predictions and decisions. Continued research and development in this area promises even greater advances and wider application across a variety of industries, from automotive and healthcare to speech and text processing. However, the challenges of interpretability and data dependency remain and require further innovation and technological advances.

Role and importance of training data

Training data is the basis on which AI models learn to recognize patterns, make predictions and take decisions. It is essential for the performance, accuracy and robustness of the developed models. Without high-quality and representative training data, the development of effective AI systems would be virtually impossible.

A key aspect of training data is its quality. High-quality training data is clean, consistent and free of errors or noise. If the data is faulty, incomplete or inconsistent, the model can learn incorrect patterns and make inaccurate predictions. The process of data pre-processing, which involves cleaning, normalizing and transforming the raw data, is therefore crucial. This process corrects errors, removes inconsistencies and converts the data into a format that is suitable for model training.

The representativeness of the training data is another critical factor. The training data must reflect the diversity and complexity of the real world to ensure that the model is able to generalize to a variety of situations. If the training data is not representative, the model may develop biases and perform poorly on new, unfamiliar data. A common problem is data bias, where certain groups or characteristics are over- or under-represented in the training data. This can lead to systematic errors and unfair predictions. It is therefore important to ensure a broad and diverse data collection that covers all relevant characteristics and scenarios.

The amount of training data also plays an important role. For complex models, especially deep learning, large amounts of data are required to optimize the parameters of the model and capture the patterns in the data. Large data sets allow the model to recognize subtle patterns and relationships, leading to better and more accurate predictions. At the same time, however, the data must also be relevant and meaningful. A large amount of irrelevant data can confuse the model and significantly increase training time without improving performance.

An important aspect of using training data is overfitting. Overfitting occurs when a model is tuned too closely to the training data and over-learns the underlying patterns of the data, including noise and randomness. This causes the model to generalize poorly on new data. To avoid overfitting, techniques such as cross-validation, regularization and the use of a separate validation dataset are used. These methods help to ensure that the model learns the general patterns in the data without relying too much on the specific details of the training data.

In addition to the quantity and quality of the data, the diversity of the data sources is also important. Different data sources can provide different perspectives and information that enrich the model and increase its robustness. For example, an image recognition model can benefit from data that comes from different camera angles, lighting conditions and resolutions. Similarly, a language model can benefit from data derived from different dialects, speaking styles and contexts. Integrating data from multiple sources can improve the model's ability to perform accurately and reliably in different real-world scenarios.

The importance of training data also extends to ethical and social aspects. As AI systems are increasingly integrated into decision-making processes that affect people's lives, it is essential that training data is free from bias and discrimination. Biased data can lead to unfair and discriminatory results that disadvantage certain groups. Therefore, it is important to conduct careful reviews and audits of training data to ensure that it is fair and representative.

Another important point is data security and data protection. In many application areas, particularly in healthcare and finance, training data contains sensitive and personal information. Protecting this data from unauthorized access and misuse is of paramount importance. This requires robust security measures and compliance with data protection regulations such as the General Data Protection Regulation (GDPR) in the European Union. Anonymization and pseudonymization of personal data are common techniques to ensure data privacy while preserving the usefulness of the data for training.

Continuously updating and improving the training data is another aspect that needs to be considered. The world is constantly changing and new data needs to be regularly incorporated into model training to ensure that the model's predictions and decisions remain relevant and up-to-date. This requires a dynamic approach where the model is continuously updated and improved with new data. This can be achieved through techniques such as online learning and incremental learning, where the model continuously learns from new data without having to retrain the entire model from scratch.

Training data therefore plays a central role in the development and performance of AI models. Its quality, quantity, representativeness and diversity are crucial for the accuracy, robustness and fairness of the models. Careful data collection, pre-processing, verification and continuous updating can overcome the challenges associated with training data and develop powerful AI systems. The ethical and safety aspects of data use must always be considered in order to create trustworthy and responsible AI solutions.

Data quality and quantity

The quality and quantity of data are other key factors that determine the success and performance of AI models.

Without high-quality and sufficient data, even the best algorithms and models will not be able to make reliable and accurate predictions or handle complex tasks. Data quality and quantity are closely linked and influence each other in many ways, and both aspects must be carefully considered to achieve optimal results.

Data quality refers to the accuracy, completeness, consistency, timeliness and relevance of the data. High-quality data must be accurate and error-free, as inaccuracies and inconsistencies can significantly affect a model's ability to recognize accurate patterns and make predictions. Completeness means that all necessary data points are present, with no gaps that could miss important information. Consistency ensures that the data is uniform across different sources and time periods, while timeliness means that the data is up to date and reflects current reality. Relevance refers to the data being relevant and meaningful to the specific task or problem the model is intended to solve.

A critical step in ensuring data quality is data pre-processing, which involves cleansing, normalizing and transforming the raw data. In this process, errors are corrected, inconsistencies are eliminated and the data is converted into a format that is suitable for model training. This step is often time-consuming and requires a deep understanding of the data source and the specific requirements of the application. Automated tools and techniques can help to make data pre-processing more efficient, but human intervention and domain knowledge remain essential.

The quantity of data is also crucial. For many machine learning models, especially deep neural networks, large amounts of data are required to optimize the parameters of the model and capture the underlying patterns in the data. Large data sets allow the model to recognize subtle and complex relationships, leading to better and more accurate predictions. A large dataset also helps to reduce the risk of overfitting, as the model is able to train on a wider variety of examples rather than clinging to specific details of the training dataset.

However, the quantity of data must be considered in the context of its quality. A large amount of irrelevant or low-quality data can confuse the model and significantly increase training time without improving performance. Therefore, it is important to ensure that the data collected is both plentiful and of high quality. This balancing act requires careful data selection and collection, critically evaluating data sources and including only the data that is relevant and useful for the specific application.

Another important aspect is the representativeness of the data. The data must reflect the diversity and complexity of the real world to ensure that the model is able to generalize to a variety of situations. If the training data is not representative, the model may develop biases and perform poorly on new, unfamiliar data. For example, a face recognition model that has been trained primarily with images of people of a particular ethnicity may perform poorly when recognizing faces of other ethnicities. To avoid such biases, the data must cover diverse and varied features and scenarios.

The relevance and quality of the data are also of great importance with regard to ethical and social aspects. Biased data can lead to unfair and discriminatory results that disadvantage certain groups. It is therefore essential that training data is carefully reviewed and audited to ensure that it is fair and representative. The protection of personal data and compliance with data protection regulations is also of paramount importance, particularly in areas such as healthcare and finance where sensitive information is processed.

Continuously updating and improving the quality and quantity of data is also crucial. The world is constantly changing, and new data must be regularly incorporated into model training to ensure that the model's predictions and decisions remain relevant and up-to-date. This requires a dynamic approach where the model is continuously updated and improved with new data. Online learning and incremental learning are techniques that allow the model to continuously learn from new data without having to retrain the entire model from scratch.

The influence of data on AI development

Data is therefore at the heart of AI development and has a significant influence on the performance, accuracy and range of applications of AI models. Their quality, quantity, diversity and representativeness determine how well a model is trained, which patterns it recognizes and how reliable its predictions and decisions are.

The quality of the data plays a central role, as described above. High-quality data is precise, consistent and free of errors or noise. Such data allows the model to learn clear and accurate patterns, leading to reliable predictions. However, if the data is flawed or incomplete, the model can learn incorrect patterns, leading to inaccurate or even harmful predictions. The process of data preprocessing, which involves cleaning and normalizing the data, is therefore of central importance. This process removes inconsistencies and converts the data into a suitable format that is optimal for model training.

The quantity of data is also crucial. Large amounts of data are necessary to reflect the complexity and diversity of the real world in the training data. Especially for deep learning and complex models, large datasets are required to effectively train the parameters of the model and recognize subtle patterns. Large datasets also help to reduce the risk of overfitting by allowing the model to learn on a wide variety of examples rather than clinging to specific details of the training data. However, quantity must always be considered in the context of quality, as large amounts of irrelevant or low-quality data can affect model performance.

The diversity of the data is another critical factor. A representative and diverse data set ensures that the model is able to generalize to different scenarios and perform well in different real-world applications. Data that includes different demographic characteristics, geographic regions, time periods and other relevant variables helps to avoid bias and distortion. If certain groups or characteristics are over- or under-represented in the training data, the model may develop systematic errors that lead to unfair or discriminatory results. Ensuring the diversity and representativeness of the data is therefore essential for the development of fair and balanced AI systems.

The influence of data on model complexity and selection is also significant. The type and structure of the available data often determine which model architectures and learning algorithms are best suited. For example, high-dimensional data, such as images or genetic sequences, require complex models such as convolutional neural networks (CNNs) or deeply nested neural networks to effectively extract and learn the relevant features. On the other hand, simpler models such as linear regression or decision trees may be sufficient if the data structure is less complex. The data thus influences the developers' decisions regarding the model architecture and the learning algorithms used.

The temporal aspect of the data also influences AI development. Data collected over longer periods of time can provide valuable information about trends and temporal patterns. Such time-dependent data is particularly relevant in areas such as economics, climate and weather forecasting and epidemiological modeling. Models trained on such data must be able to account for temporal dependencies and developments, which often requires the use of specialized model architectures such as Recurrent Neural Networks (RNNs) or Long Short-Term Memory (LSTM) networks.

Data also influences the speed and efficiency of model development and deployment. Comprehensive and well-organized data sets enable more efficient training processes and accelerate development cycles. If the data is easily accessible and well documented, developers can create prototypes faster and improve models iteratively. In many cases, techniques such as transfer learning are used, where pre-trained models on large data sets are used as a starting point to reduce training time and the amount of data required.

The origin and ethics of data are also important influences on AI development. The source of the data and the way in which it was collected influence the quality and reliability of the models. Data that comes from trustworthy and ethically unobjectionable sources helps to strengthen trust in the AI systems developed. At the same time, data protection and data security must be guaranteed, especially when personal or sensitive information is involved. Compliance with data protection regulations such as the General Data Protection Regulation (GDPR) in the European Union is crucial to protect the rights of data subjects and avoid legal risks.

Model complexity and its effects

Model complexity is another key issue in artificial intelligence and machine learning, as it has an impact on the performance, generalizability and interpretability of AI models. A complex model can include a variety of parameters and deeply nested structures that allow it to capture high-dimensional and non-linear relationships in the data. This capability is particularly valuable in application areas such as image and speech recognition, natural language processing and the prediction of complex patterns in large data sets.

A higher model complexity enables an AI system to recognize finer and more detailed patterns in the data. This is particularly useful in situations where the underlying relationships between variables are complex and non-linear. By utilizing multiple layers of neurons in deep neural networks, a complex model can extract abstract features from the raw data and transform these features into increasingly abstract representations. For example, a deep neural network can recognize simple edges and textures in an image in the lower layers and identify complex objects such as faces or vehicles in the higher layers.

However, the ability to learn complex patterns also carries the aforementioned risk of overfitting. An overfitted model may perform excellently on the training data but perform poorly on new, unknown data because it cannot transfer the specific details of the training data to general cases.

Model complexity also has an impact on training and calculation time. More complex models require more computing resources and longer training times to find the optimal parameters. This requires powerful hardware, such as GPUs or TPUs, and can make the development and implementation of AI models time-consuming and costly. In addition, training complex models requires large amounts of data to ensure that the model has enough examples to learn the underlying patterns. This can be a challenge when high-quality and representative data is difficult to obtain.

The generalizability of a model, i.e. its ability to be transferred to new, unknown data, is also influenced by model complexity. A model that is too simple cannot fully capture the complexity of the data and leads to underfitting, where the model is unable to learn the relevant patterns in the data. A model that is too complex, on the other hand, may be overfitting and impair the ability to generalize. The key is to find the right balance between complexity and simplicity to develop a model that both describes the training data well and is applicable to new data.

Another important aspect of model complexity is interpretability. Simple models such as linear regressions or decision trees are easy to interpret as the relationships between the input variables and the outputs are clear and understandable. Complex models, especially deep neural networks, on the other hand, are often known as black box models as their internal decision-making processes are difficult to understand. This can be problematic when the model's decisions are critical or security-relevant, such as in medicine, the judiciary or the financial sector. Research into the explainability and transparency of AI models, also known as Explainable AI (XAI), aims to better understand the internal mechanisms of complex models and make them comprehensible.

The robustness and reliability of AI models are also closely linked to their complexity. Complex models can be susceptible to small changes in the input data that lead to large changes in the output. This is particularly problematic in safety-critical applications where reliable and stable predictions are required. Techniques such as adversarial training, where the model is trained on specially designed inputs that aim to confuse it, can help improve the robustness of complex models.

Finally, model complexity also has ethical and social implications. The use of complex, difficult-to-understand models in decision-making processes can affect the trust of users and society in AI systems. It is important that developers and users of AI systems consider the impact of model complexity on the transparency and fairness of decisions and take steps to ensure that models are ethical and socially acceptable.

Simplicity vs. complexity

The tension between simplicity and complexity in model development is naturally another key issue in artificial intelligence and machine learning. Both approaches have their own advantages and disadvantages and significantly influence the performance, generalizability, interpretability and efficiency of AI models. A deeper understanding of this area of tension is crucial for the development of optimal solutions that meet the specific requirements and challenges of different application areas.

Simplicity in model development usually means that the model has relatively few parameters and a manageable structure. Simple models such as linear regressions, decision trees or logistic regressions are often easy to understand and interpret. They provide clear insights into the relationships between the input and output variables and make it possible to understand the model's decision-making processes. This is particularly important in areas where transparency and traceability are crucial, such as medicine, justice or the financial sector. Simple models are also faster to train and implement, require fewer computing resources and are often more robust to small changes in the input data.

However, simple models also have their limitations. They often cannot fully capture the complexity of the data, especially if the underlying relationships between the variables are non-linear or very complex. In such cases, a simple model can lead to underfitting, where the model fails to recognize the relevant patterns in the data and thus makes inaccurate predictions. This is particularly problematic in complex tasks such as image recognition, natural language processing or predicting market movements, where the data is often high-dimensional and highly non-linear.

Complex models, such as deep learning and multilayer neural networks, provide the ability to capture high-dimensional and nonlinear relationships in the data. They can extract abstract features from the raw data and transform these features into increasingly complex representations, leading to more accurate and powerful predictions. This is particularly valuable in application areas such as image and speech recognition, natural language processing and the prediction of complex patterns in large data sets. Due to their ability to recognize subtle and complex patterns, complex models can deliver better results than simple models, especially in data-driven and dynamic environments.

However, the increased model complexity also brings challenges. Complex models are often more prone to overfitting, where they learn the training data too accurately and also capture the noise and randomness in the data. This can lead to poor generalizability, as the model cannot transfer the specific details of the training data to general cases. To avoid overfitting, techniques such as regularization, cross-validation and the use of dropout layers must be used. However, these techniques increase the complexity of the training process and require additional computational resources and expertise.

Another problem with complex models is their broad interpretability. Deep neural networks and other complex models are often known as black box models, as their internal decision-making processes are difficult to understand. This can be problematic if the model's decisions are critical or safety-relevant. There is ongoing research into the explainability and transparency of AI models in order to better understand the internal mechanisms of complex models and make them comprehensible. Explainable AI (XAI) aims to develop models that are not only efficient, but also transparent and understandable.

The choice between simplicity and complexity is often a trade-off that depends on the specific requirements and objectives of the application area. In many cases, a hybrid approach that combines elements of both approaches can deliver the best results. For example, a simple model can be used as a starting point to identify basic patterns and provide an initial assessment. A more complex model can then be used to perform deeper and more detailed analysis and make more accurate predictions.

The complexity of the data and the availability of computing resources are also important factors that influence the choice between simplicity and complexity. For high-dimensional and complex data, such as images, videos or genetic sequences, complex models are often essential to effectively extract and learn the relevant features. For less complex data or in scenarios with limited computational resources, a simpler model may be the better choice as it is faster to train and implement and is often sufficient to provide useful results.

The ethical and societal implications of model complexity should also not be overlooked. Complex models can be difficult to understand and control, which can affect user and societal trust in AI systems. It is important that developers and users of AI systems consider the impact of model complexity on the transparency and fairness of decisions and take steps to ensure that models are ethical and socially acceptable.

Over-adaptation and under-adaptation

Overfitting and underfitting are two fundamental problems that can occur in model development in machine learning, as already described. They affect the ability of a model to recognize patterns in the data and generalize them to new, unknown data. An understanding of these phenomena is crucial in order to develop models that perform well on both training data and new data.

Overfitting occurs when a model learns the training data too accurately and also captures the noise and randomness in the data. As a result, the model performs very well on the training data but performs poorly on new, unknown data because it cannot transfer the specific details of the training data to general cases. Overfitting is particularly problematic in complex models with many parameters, such as deep neural networks, which have high flexibility and are able to learn very specific patterns. Various techniques are used to avoid overfitting. Regularization is a method that adds additional information to force the model to learn simpler and less specific patterns. There are different types of regularization, such as L1 and L2 regularization, which add penalties for large model parameters to reduce the complexity of the model. Cross-validation is another technique where the training set is divided into multiple parts and the model is trained and validated multiple times to ensure that it generalizes well. Dropout, a technique used in neural networks, randomly deactivates a number of neurons during training to reduce the model's dependence on specific neurons and increase robustness.

Underfitting occurs when a model does not learn the underlying patterns in the training data well enough. This results in the model performing poorly on both the training data and new data. Underfitting often occurs when the model is too simple and does not have enough capacity to capture the complexity of the data. This can happen if the model has too few parameters or if the algorithm used is not complex enough to learn the underlying relationships in the data. A simple example is linear regression, which is not able to capture non-linear relationships. To avoid underfitting, the model needs to be made more complex. This can be done by using more complex algorithms, adding more parameters or layers in neural networks, or by providing additional and relevant features that the model can learn.

The balance between overfitting and underfitting is crucial for the development of a good generalizing model. A well-generalizing model is able to learn the underlying patterns in the training data and apply these patterns to new data. This requires careful selection and configuration of the model, including choosing the right model architecture, the right amount of training data, and the right techniques to avoid overfitting and underfitting.

Another important aspect of avoiding overfitting and underfitting is the selection and pre-processing of the data. High quality, representative and diverse training data is crucial for the development of a good generalizing model. Data pre-processing, including cleaning, normalizing and transforming the data, plays an important role in ensuring that the model learns relevant and useful patterns.

The size of the training data set is also important. Large data sets help to reduce the effects of noise and improve the generalization ability of the model. However, if only limited data is available, techniques such as data augmentation can be used to artificially generate additional training data. Data augmentation involves creating new data points through transformations such as rotation, scaling or warping of existing data, which is particularly useful in image processing.

Choosing the right metrics to evaluate model performance is also critical. It is important to evaluate not only the performance on the training data, but also the performance on a separate set of test data that was not used during the training process. This helps to ensure that the model has generalized well and not just learned the specific details of the training data. Metrics such as accuracy, precision, recall and the F1 score can be used to comprehensively evaluate the performance of the model.

Phenomena of "psychoses" in AI

Description of misbehavior in AI systems

The phenomenon of "psychosis" in artificial intelligence refers metaphorically to situations in which AI systems exhibit behavior that appears unpredictable, irrational or illogical.

This type of misbehavior can be caused by a variety of factors, including faulty data processing, algorithmic problems or technical malfunctions, etc. Such anomalies cause the AI to produce results or actions that deviate greatly from the user's expectations. Although AI systems have no consciousness or emotional states and therefore cannot be truly psychotic in the medical sense, the metaphor provides a vivid way of describing the way in which and why AI systems sometimes produce unpredictable and irrational results.

Misbehavior in AI systems can be defined as any type of response or outcome that deviates from intended or expected functions and is potentially harmful or confusing. These anomalies can occur in a variety of ways, including illogical responses, unpredictable actions or faulty decision making.

Examples of unexpected or incorrect behavior

Biased decisions (bias)

Unexpected or erroneous behavior in artificial intelligence systems can manifest itself in many different ways and has far-reaching implications, especially when it comes to biased decisions or bias.

A classic example of unexpected or incorrect behavior is voice assistants that give confusing or illogical answers to simple questions. A user might ask the voice assistant for the weather forecast and instead of a clear weather forecast, the assistant might respond with an absurd or incoherent statement. This behavior can be due to problems in natural language processing, such as misunderstandings in the interpretation of the user's request or errors in the processing of contextual information. Such errors are often caused by insufficient training data that does not cover all possible variations and nuances of human language.

Another example is the behavior of autonomous vehicles, which can perform unexpected or dangerous maneuvers. Autonomous vehicles rely on a variety of sensors and algorithms to understand their environment and navigate safely. However, if a vehicle suddenly changes lanes or brakes abruptly due to faulty sensor data or incorrect interpretation of traffic situations, this can lead to dangerous situations. Such problems can be caused by insufficient or distorted training data that does not adequately represent certain traffic situations, or by errors in the algorithms used for processing and decision-making.

In medical diagnostics, AI systems can also exhibit unexpected or erroneous behavior if they make incorrect diagnoses or suggest inaccurate treatment plans. An AI system trained on imaging data to detect diseases such as cancer could provide false positives or false negatives due to insufficient or biased training data. This not only has medical consequences, but also ethical and legal implications, as patients may receive unnecessary treatment or be denied necessary treatment. The quality and variety of the training data is crucial here to ensure that the model is able to correctly recognize and diagnose the relevant patterns.

Another example is lending, where AI systems are used to assess the creditworthiness of applicants. If the training data contains historical distortions, such as a systematic disadvantage for certain social or ethnic groups, the AI system can adopt these distortions and reproduce them in its decisions. This leads to unequal treatment of applicants, with certain groups systematically receiving lower credit scores. Such a bias can have a significant economic and social impact and undermine trust in the fairness of AI systems.

In criminal justice, for example, AI systems used to predict the likelihood of offenders reoffending can also make incorrect or biased decisions. If the training data contains biases, such as higher recidivism rates for certain ethnic groups due to historical discrimination, the

AI system can adopt and reinforce these biases. This leads to unfair and discriminatory decisions that can have a significant impact on the lives of those affected. Such systems must therefore be carefully developed, monitored and reviewed to ensure that they are fair and equitable.

The cause of many of these problems often lies in the training data, which may not only be incorrect or inadequate, but may also contain systematic biases and distortions. These biases can be consciously or unconsciously present in the data and are adopted and reinforced by the AI system. An example of this is recruitment, where AI systems use historical data to assess the suitability of applicants. If the historical data contains a bias towards certain genders, ethnicities or age groups, the AI system can adopt this bias and systematically disadvantage certain applicant groups.

Algorithmic problems can also lead to unexpected or erroneous behavior. Complex algorithms used for deep learning and neural networks can have unexpected interactions between the different layers and neurons, leading to unpredictable results. These problems are often difficult to diagnose and fix because the internal decision-making processes of such models are complex and opaque. This poses a challenge for the interpretability and explainability of AI models, which is particularly important in safety-critical and ethically sensitive applications.

Technical faults such as hardware errors, software bugs or network problems can also lead to unexpected or incorrect behavior. A hardware failure in the GPU that performs the calculations or a software bug in the data processing routine can cause the system to produce incorrect or illogical results. Such technical problems require robust error detection and correction mechanisms to ensure the reliability and stability of the AI system.

Misinterpretations and hallucinations

Misinterpretations and hallucinations in artificial intelligence systems are phenomena in which the AI delivers results that deviate greatly from the expected reality.

Misinterpretations occur when an AI system incorrectly analyzes input data and reaches the wrong conclusions as a result. One example of this is image processing, where an AI system incorrectly identifies an object in an image as another object. A self-driving car could, for example, interpret a shadow on the road as an obstacle and brake abruptly even though there is no real obstacle. Such misinterpretations can be due to incorrect or insufficient training data that has not adequately prepared the system for different scenarios. Algorithmic weaknesses or limitations in sensor data processing can also contribute to such misinterpretations.

Hallucinations in AI systems refer to the generation of content or results that have no basis in the input data. These phenomena are particularly common in generative models such as those used to produce text, images or other creative content.

A well-known example is generative adversarial networks, which can generate realistic-looking images. However, if such models work incorrectly, they can produce images that are surreal or bizarre and contain features that do not occur in reality. A text generation model could respond to a simple input by producing incoherent or absurdly long text that makes no sense.

The causes of misinterpretations and hallucinations are manifold. One common cause is the quality and variety of the training data. Algorithmic problems also play a significant role in the emergence of these phenomena. Complex models such as deep neural networks have many parameters and layers that interact with each other. If these models are not properly configured or optimized, they can have unexpected interactions that lead to incorrect results. For example, a deep neural network used for image processing could produce strange artifacts in the deep layers based on overly complex or misunderstood patterns.

Technical faults, such as hardware errors, software bugs or network problems, can also lead to misinterpretations and hallucinations. A defective sensor in an autonomous vehicle could provide incorrect data that the AI system interprets incorrectly. A software bug could cause a text generation model to produce incoherent or nonsensical texts. Such technical problems require robust error detection and correction mechanisms to ensure the reliability and stability of the AI system.

Comparison with human psychoses

Comparing AI misbehavior to human psychosis offers an interesting perspective to better understand the workings and challenges of artificial intelligence. While there are important differences, there are also some notable similarities that make this metaphor both useful and insightful.

Human psychoses are characterized by profound disturbances in perception, thinking and reality. People suffering from psychosis may experience hallucinations (perceptions without external stimuli) and delusions (false beliefs). These symptoms often result from biochemical imbalances or structural abnormalities in the brain.

In comparison, misbehavior in AI systems is the result of faulty data processing, algorithmic problems or technical malfunctions. Despite the fundamental differences in the origin and nature of the two phenomena, there are interesting parallels that can explain and illustrate this metaphor.

One of the most notable similarities between human psychosis and AI misbehavior is the loss of connection to reality. In humans with psychosis, the perception of reality can be severely distorted, leading to hallucinations and delusions.

Similarly, incorrect data processing or algorithmic problems can cause an AI to produce results that deviate greatly from reality. For example, an image classification algorithm could identify an image of an apple as a dog, which is tantamount to a kind of "hallucination", as the AI sees an object that does not exist.

Another point of comparison is the unpredictability and irrationality of behavior. In human psychosis, actions and thoughts are often unpredictable and illogical, similar to an AI that responds to certain inputs with incoherent or incomprehensible results. A voice assistant might respond to a simple question about the weather with a confusing answer about philosophical concepts, which seems just as unpredictable and irrational to the user as the behavior of a person with psychosis.

Despite these parallels, there are of course also significant differences that need to be taken into account. Human psychoses result from biological and psychological processes that are linked to conscious perception, emotions and individual experiences. AI systems, on the other hand, are purely mechanistic and data-driven, without consciousness or emotions. Their "misbehaviors" are the result of faulty algorithms, insufficient data or technical malfunctions and have no subjective experience or intentionality.

The causes of misbehavior also vary. In human psychoses, biochemical imbalances, genetic predispositions and environmental factors all play a role. In AI systems, it is often the quality and representativeness of the training data as well as the accuracy and robustness of the algorithms that influence behavior. An AI model can make biased decisions if it is trained on data that contains systematic biases. Such biases can cause the model to make discriminatory or unfair decisions, similar to the delusions of a psychotic person based on false beliefs.

The resolution and treatment of these problems also differ. Human psychoses often require medical interventions, such as psychotherapy and medication, to restore the biochemical balance in the brain and alleviate the psychological symptoms. Often this is not successful at all.

In AI systems, misbehaviour requires measures such as cleaning and improving data quality, optimizing algorithms and implementing robust monitoring and maintenance mechanisms. While human psychosis requires a deep understanding of the individual and biochemical background, correcting AI misbehavior requires technical expertise and systematic approaches to troubleshooting.

Another difference lies in the scalability of the solutions. Human psychoses need to be treated individually, as each person has unique symptoms and causes. With AI systems, systematic improvements in data quality and algorithm architecture can potentially be applied to many applications and models simultaneously. A single improved model or corrected data pipeline can be used in many different contexts, increasing the efficiency and effectiveness of the solutions.

The ethical implications are also an important point of differentiation. In the treatment of human psychosis, the focus is on the well-being and autonomy of the person affected, which requires complex ethical considerations. In AI malpractice, the ethical issues focus on the fairness, transparency and accountability of algorithms and systems. It is crucial to ensure that AI systems do not make discriminatory or unethical decisions and that users understand how and why certain decisions are made.

Thus, it can be said that comparing AI misbehavior to human psychosis provides a vivid metaphor to better understand the challenges and risks of AI systems. Although there are important differences in the causes, nature and treatment methods, the parallels help to illustrate the potential dangers and the need for careful development and monitoring of AI systems. A deep understanding of these phenomena can help to develop more robust, reliable and ethical AI solutions that meet society's expectations and requirements.

Causes of "psychosis" in AI

Incorrect or contradictory training data

The causes of "psychosis" in artificial intelligence can be manifold, but one of the main causes is incorrect or contradictory training data.

These data problems can significantly influence the behavior of AI systems and lead to unpredictable or irrational results. Training data forms the basis on which AI models learn to recognize patterns and make decisions. If this data is not of high quality, the resulting models can be correspondingly flawed and unreliable.

Incorrect training data can arise in various ways. One common reason is the manual input of data, which can lead to typing errors, incorrect entries or incomplete data sets. In large datasets that come from different sources, inconsistencies and errors can go unnoticed and have a negative impact on model performance. An example would be a medical diagnosis dataset that contains incorrect diagnoses or incomplete patient information due to manual errors. When an AI model is trained on such data, it can result in incorrect diagnoses or treatment plans, which can have serious consequences for the patients concerned.

Inconsistent training data occurs when the data contains inconsistent information that confuses the model. This can happen if the data comes from different sources that use different standards and formats, or if it has been collected over a long period of time and reflects changes in the underlying processes or systems. For example, a data set on customer reviews of products could contain both positive and negative reviews of the same product without clearly identifying the conditions under which the reviews were given. An AI model trained on such data may struggle to provide a consistent rating and make inconsistent or contradictory recommendations.

Another aspect of erroneous training data is the bias that may be present in the data. These biases can be systematic errors in the data caused by historical inequalities or biases. When an AI model is trained on such biased data, it can adopt these biases and reproduce them in its predictions and decisions. A typical example is the bias in job application data, where historical data reflects a systematic disadvantage of certain groups. An AI system that is trained on such data could unconsciously reinforce these disadvantages and systematically exclude certain applicant groups.

The quality of the training data can also be impaired by insufficient representativeness. If the data does not reflect the entire diversity of the real world, the model can only generalize to a limited extent. This means that it performs well on the training data but fails on new, unknown data. An example would be a facial recognition algorithm that has been trained mainly with images of people of a certain ethnicity. Such a model may have difficulty correctly recognizing faces of other ethnicities, leading to erroneous or discriminatory results. These problems can have significant societal and ethical implications, especially if the AI systems are used in safety-critical or socially sensitive applications.

Incorrect or contradictory training data can also result from inadequate data preparation and pre-processing. The process of data pre-processing includes steps such as data cleaning, normalization and transformation to ensure that the data is in a suitable form for training. If these steps are not carried out carefully, incorrect or incomplete data can be incorporated into the model and affect its performance. For example, missing values in a dataset due to improper padding could lead to incorrect assumptions that mislead the model.

In addition, the dynamics of the real world can lead to problems if the training data is not updated regularly. If a model is trained on outdated data that does not reflect current conditions, it may misbehave when confronted with new, changed data. This is particularly relevant in fast-moving areas such as financial market analysis or the fashion industry, where trends and conditions are constantly changing. An AI model that is not regularly fed with up-to-date data can make erroneous predictions that are no longer relevant or correct.

Data quality and diversity

The quality and diversity of data play a central role in avoiding "psychosis" in AI systems, which can manifest itself in unpredictable, irrational or illogical results.

When data is of poor quality or insufficiently diverse, this can have a profound impact on the model's ability to make accurate and reliable predictions. These problems can occur at different levels and their effects can be far-reaching and complex.

Data quality refers to the accuracy, consistency, completeness and relevance of the data used to train AI models. High-quality data is accurate and free of errors or inconsistencies. However, if the data is incorrect or incomplete, the model can learn incorrect patterns and make inaccurate predictions.

A classic example is medical diagnosis, where incomplete or incorrect patient records can lead to incorrect diagnoses. In the financial sector, incorrect data could lead to wrong investment decisions, which could result in significant financial losses.

Another aspect of data quality is the consistency of the data. If the data comes from different sources and uses different standards or formats, inconsistencies can arise that confuse the model. This can lead to the model making contradictory or illogical decisions. For example, a customer preference prediction model may struggle to deliver consistent results if the underlying data is formatted differently or is partially incomplete. These inconsistencies make it difficult for the model to recognize clear patterns and make correct predictions.

Data quality is also influenced by distortions or biases that may be present in the data. These distortions can result from historical inequalities or systematic errors and are often adopted and amplified by AI models.

For example, a recruitment algorithm based on historical data could unconsciously reproduce existing gender or racial biases, leading to unfair or discriminatory hiring decisions. Such biases are particularly problematic as they are difficult to detect and correct, but can have significant social and ethical implications.

In addition to quality, the diversity of data plays an important role in avoiding "psychosis" in AI systems. Data diversity refers to the range of data that covers different demographic groups, geographical regions, time periods and other relevant variables. A lack of diversity in the training data can result in the model not being able to adequately represent the diversity of the real world. This leads to poor generalization ability of the model, which must be able to respond to a variety of scenarios and conditions.

One example of the need for data diversity is facial recognition technology. If the training data consists mainly of images of people of a particular ethnicity, the model may have difficulty correctly recognizing faces of people of other ethnicities. This can lead to a higher error rate and discriminatory results. Similar problems occur in speech recognition when the training data does not include different accents and dialects. The model may have difficulty understanding speakers with different linguistic backgrounds, resulting in a poorer user experience.

The combination of poor data quality and insufficient data variety can lead to particularly serious errors in AI systems. Models trained on such data tend to learn incorrect patterns and produce illogical or unpredictable results. These "psychoses" in AI systems can take the form of hallucinations, where the model generates content or results that have no basis in the input data. For example, a text generation model might respond to a simple query by producing incoherent or absurdly long text that makes no sense. Such results are not only confusing, but can also undermine user confidence in the AI technology.

Overfitting and model complexity

Overfitting and model complexity are two closely related concepts in the field of machine learning that significantly influence the performance and generalizability of AI models.

Overfitting occurs when a model learns the training data too accurately, including noise and randomness, resulting in poor performance on new, unknown data. Model complexity plays a central role here, as more complex models have a greater capacity to capture the details of the training data, which has both advantages and disadvantages.

A model is said to be overfitted when it learns the specific patterns and randomness in the training data so well that it can no longer generalize to new data. This means that the model not only captures the underlying, relevant patterns in the data, but also the noise and peculiarities of the training data. As a result, the model may perform extremely well on the training data, but when validated or applied to new data, it performs significantly worse. This is particularly problematic as the goal of machine learning is to develop models that generalize well on new, unknown data.

Model complexity refers to the number of parameters and the structure of the model. A simple model has fewer parameters and a simpler structure, while a complex model may have many parameters and a deeply nested structure. Deep neural networks are an example of very complex models that are able to capture high-dimensional and non-linear relationships in the data. While such models have the potential to be very powerful, they are also more prone to overfitting as they have enough capacity to learn the training data almost perfectly, including the noise and randomness.

The main cause of overfitting is the excessive flexibility and capacity of the model in relation to the quantity and quality of the available training data. If a model has too many parameters compared to the number of data points, it can learn the training data too accurately. This results in the model not being able to distinguish between relevant patterns and random noise. An example of this would be a deep neural network that is trained with a relatively small number of data points. The network can adapt the data points so well that it can predict the training data perfectly, but it will perform poorly on new data because it has learned the noise of the training data.

There are several techniques to avoid overfitting and control model complexity. One common method is regularization, which introduces additional constraints or penalties on the model parameters to limit their values and thereby reduce the complexity of the model. Commonly used regularization techniques include L1 and L2 regularization, which help to keep the model parameters smaller and more parsimonious, reducing the risk of overfitting.

Another important tool for avoiding overfitting is cross-validation. In cross-validation, the training set is divided into several parts and the model is trained and validated multiple times by using one part at a time as the validation set and the remaining parts as the training set. This helps to better assess and improve the generalization ability of the model as the model is tested on different subsets of the data. It provides a more robust estimate of model performance and helps to reduce the risk of overfitting.

Dropout is a specific technique used in deep neural networks to prevent overfitting. In dropout, randomly selected neurons are deactivated during training, which prevents the model from becoming too dependent on certain paths and connections. This forces the model to learn more redundant and robust features that generalize better. Dropout reduces the model's dependence on specific neurons and connections and helps improve generalization ability.

Choosing the right model complexity is a balancing act between underfitting and overfitting. Underfitting occurs when the model is too simple and does not have the ability to capture the underlying patterns in the data. This leads to poor performance on both the training data and new data. A model that is too simple cannot capture the complexity of the data and therefore provides inaccurate predictions. It is important to choose a model that is complex enough to capture the relevant patterns in the data, but not so complex that it learns the noise and randomness of the training data.

A good understanding of the data and the underlying problem is crucial to choose the right model complexity and avoid overfitting. It is important to analyze the data thoroughly to understand its structure and properties, and then choose a model that matches this structure. In addition, techniques such as regularization, cross-validation and dropout should be used to control model complexity and reduce the risk of overfitting.

In practice, this often requires iterative experimentation and fine-tuning. Developers need to test different model architectures and hyperparameter combinations to find the best balance between complexity and generalizability. This includes testing and validating models on separate data sets to ensure that they generalize well to new, unknown data. Careful planning, continuous monitoring and adjustment of models can minimize the risk of overfitting and maximize generalization ability.

Data bias and its effects

Types of bias (cultural, demographic)

Data bias is another critical problem in the field of artificial intelligence that can have a profound impact on the performance and fairness of AI systems. These biases arise when the data used to train a model is not representative of the actual diversity and complexity of the real world. Such biases can cause AI systems to produce unpredictable or illogical results, often described as AI "psychosis". Different types of bias, including cultural and demographic biases, contribute to these problems and have different effects.

Cultural bias occurs when the training data is culturally biased and therefore favors certain cultural norms, values or practices. This can lead to AI systems systematically disadvantaging or misunderstanding certain cultural groups. An example of cultural bias could be a language model that has been trained primarily with data from a specific language culture and has difficulty correctly interpreting language variants or slang from other cultures. This can lead to misunderstandings, incorrect translations or inappropriate responses that disadvantage or annoy users from underrepresented cultures.

Demographic bias, on the other hand, occurs when the training data is demographically biased and certain population groups are overrepresented or underrepresented. This can lead to AI systems making decisions that systematically disadvantage certain demographic groups. A classic example of demographic bias is facial recognition technology. If a model is trained primarily with images of people from a certain ethnicity or age group, it may have difficulty correctly recognizing faces of people from other ethnicities or age groups. This leads to higher error rates and potentially discriminatory results that can significantly disadvantage the people concerned.

The impact of data bias on the performance and fairness of AI systems is significant. Biased data causes the model to learn incorrect or inaccurate patterns, leading to erroneous or unfair predictions and decisions. This can have serious consequences in many areas, from medical diagnostics to lending and criminal justice. In medical diagnostics, a biased model could miss or misdiagnose certain diseases in certain populations because the training data does not adequately represent these groups. In lending, certain demographic groups could systematically receive lower credit scores because the historical data contains biases that the model inherits and amplifies. In criminal justice, certain ethnic groups may be assigned higher recidivism probabilities because the model is based on biased data that reflects historical inequities.

These biases not only lead to inaccurate or unfair results, but also undermine users' trust in AI systems. When users realize that an AI system systematically makes biased or discriminatory decisions, trust in the technology and its applications decreases. This can significantly affect the acceptance and success of AI systems and lead to legal and regulatory challenges.

Case studies of AI systems with bias problems

Bias in AI systems is a widespread problem that has a significant impact on various applications and industries. There are several well-documented case studies that illustrate the risks and challenges that can arise from biased data and models. These examples show how bias can lead to discriminatory and unfair results and emphasize the need for careful monitoring and corrective mechanisms in AI development.

A well-known example is the Correctional Offender Management Profiling for Alternative Sanctions (COMPAS) system, which has been used in the US to predict offenders' likelihood of recidivism. Research, particularly an analysis by ProPublica in 2016, showed that the COMPAS system systematically predicted higher recidivism probabilities for black defendants compared to white defendants, even when actual recidivism rates were comparable. This bias resulted from the underlying data reflecting historical disparities and biases. The result was unfair treatment of minorities that raised serious ethical and legal concerns and undermined confidence in the use of such systems in the criminal justice system.

Another case study is Amazon's facial recognition system, Rekognition, which is used by several law enforcement agencies. Studies, including one by the MIT Media Lab, showed that Rekognition had significant error rates in recognizing the faces of women and people with dark skin. These discrepancies were attributed to biases in the training data, which predominantly contained images of white men. Such biases in facial recognition systems can lead to false identifications and unfair treatment, especially in safety-critical applications such as law enforcement.

Another prominent example is Amazon's recruitment algorithm, which was developed to evaluate CVs and identify suitable candidates for job vacancies. It was found that the algorithm systematically disadvantaged female applicants. This was because the model was trained on historical data that reflected a bias towards men, as the technology industry has historically been male-dominated. The algorithm learned to favor certain terms and experiences typically associated with male applicants, resulting in a discriminatory selection of candidates. Amazon eventually stopped using this tool after the biases were discovered.

Another example of bias in AI systems is Apple Card's credit scoring algorithm, which is operated by Goldman Sachs. Reports in 2019 indicated that the algorithm systematically assigned women lower credit limits than their male counterparts, even when both had similar financial profiles. This led to public controversy and an investigation by regulators. The biases in credit scores were attributed to historical data and models that contained gender bias, highlighting the far-reaching impact of bias in financial services.

There are also examples of bias in AI systems in medical diagnostics. One well-known example is an algorithm that was developed to assess the need for additional examinations in patients with respiratory diseases. Studies showed that the model was less accurate for patients with dark skin color because the training data came predominantly from patients with light skin color. This bias led to unequal treatment and potentially poorer health outcomes for underrepresented groups. Such examples emphasize the need for diversified and representative training data to develop fair and accurate medical algorithms.

Another case study concerns language models such as GPT-3, which was developed by OpenAI. Research has shown that the model can generate certain racist, sexist and other discriminatory content based on the data on which it was trained. These biases reflect the biases present in the vast text corpora from which the model learns. The potential implications are far-reaching, as such language models are used in various applications, from chatbots to automated content generation tools, and thus risk propagating and amplifying these biases.

These case studies illustrate the diverse effects of bias in AI systems. They show that biases in training data and models can lead to discriminatory and unfair results that have far-reaching ethical, legal and social consequences. Careful data selection, regular checks and validation as well as the development and implementation of bias correction algorithms are necessary to avoid and eliminate these problems. In addition, awareness-raising and training of developers and decision-makers is crucial to create awareness of the potential risks and impacts of bias and to ensure that AI systems are used fairly and responsibly.

Susceptibility to incorrect entries

The susceptibility of AI systems to incorrect inputs is another key cause of the phenomenon of "psychosis" in AI, where the behavior of the AI appears unpredictable, irrational or illogical. This vulnerability means that even minor errors or deviations in the input data can cause the model to produce incorrect or bizarre results. This vulnerability is particularly problematic in safety-critical applications where accurate and reliable predictions are crucial.

Incorrect inputs can come from various sources. For example, sensors that supply data to the AI system can be faulty and generate incorrect or distorted information. This is particularly relevant in areas such as autonomous vehicle technology, where sensors such as cameras, lidar and radar continuously collect data about the environment. A small error in one of these sensors, such as a faulty calibration or a dirty lens, can lead to false perceptions. An autonomous vehicle could interpret a harmless shadow as an obstacle and brake suddenly, which can lead to dangerous situations. This shows how sensitively such systems can react to incorrect inputs.

Another example is image processing, where the smallest changes in pixel values can significantly affect the results of a model. An image classification model could arrive at incorrect or absurd predictions due to noise or slight changes in the image. This could be caused by various factors, such as the compression of the image, changes in lighting or random pixel noise. An image of a dog could suddenly be classified as a cat just because the image has been slightly modified. This sensitivity shows that the model is not robust enough to deal with such variations, leading to unpredictable results.

Text-processing AI systems are also susceptible to incorrect input. A small typographical error or unusual wording can cause the model to misinterpret the context or meaning of a text. A voice assistant could respond to a misspelled or incomplete query with an inappropriate or meaningless response. This type of misinterpretation can be particularly frustrating for users and undermine trust in the technology.

Incorrect inputs can also be caused by malicious attacks, so-called adversarial attacks. This involves deliberately making small changes to the input data in order to deceive the model and provoke incorrect predictions. For example, pixels in an image could be manipulated so that the model recognizes a stop sign as a give way sign, which can lead to potentially dangerous situations. This type of attack shows how easily incorrect inputs can undermine the robustness and reliability of a model.

Another problem is the inability of many models to process contextual information. A model that is unable to adequately consider the context of an input can easily be confused by atypical or erroneous data. For example, an AI system for analyzing medical data could interpret symptoms and test results without the clinical context and thus make incorrect diagnoses. A medical algorithm could classify an unusual but harmless symptom as a serious condition simply because the input data is not complete or contextually appropriate.

The effects of this vulnerability are far-reaching. In safety-critical applications, incorrect inputs can lead to dangerous situations that endanger the safety of people. In medical diagnostics, they can lead to incorrect diagnoses and treatment plans, affecting the health and wellbeing of patients. In financial applications, faulty inputs can lead to incorrect predictions and investment decisions, which can cause significant financial losses. These problems underline the need to improve the robustness and reliability of AI systems.

Various measures are required to reduce this susceptibility to incorrect input. Careful data pre-processing is crucial to minimize noise and errors in the input data. This includes techniques such as filtering and normalizing the data as well as implementing algorithms for error detection and correction. The development and implementation of robust models that are less sensitive to small changes in the input data is also crucial. This includes techniques such as data augmentation, regularization and the use of robust model architectures that improve generalization capability.

Another important approach is the continuous monitoring and validation of the models during operation. Models should be checked regularly to ensure that they work robustly and reliably even under changed conditions and with new data. This includes implementing mechanisms to detect and correct misbehavior and adapting the models to new data and conditions.

Finally, training and raising awareness among developers and decision-makers is crucial. It is important that all stakeholders understand the potential risks and impact of incorrect inputs and are able to take appropriate action to improve the robustness and reliability of models. This includes training and guidelines for developing robust and reliable AI systems, as well as establishing interdisciplinary teams that bring different perspectives and expertise to the table.

Importance of robustness for reliability

The robustness of an AI system is crucial to its reliability and plays a central role in avoiding "psychosis" in AI. Robustness is the ability of a model to perform stably and consistently under different conditions, including when confronted with unexpected inputs, noise or other disturbances. A robust AI system can respond effectively to variations in the data and provide reliable results even under uncertain or varying conditions. This is particularly important to ensure confidence in AI systems and support their use in critical applications.

A robust AI system is less prone to errors and can make more reliable predictions, even if the input data is incorrect or incomplete. This is crucial because the quality of input data can vary in many real-world applications. Sensors can provide erroneous data, users can make input errors, and environmental conditions can change. A robust system can overcome these challenges and provide stable performance, minimizing the risk of misbehavior and unpredictable results.

The importance of robustness is clearly evident in autonomous vehicle technology. Autonomous vehicles depend on making precise and reliable decisions in real time in order to navigate safely. A robust model can handle small errors in the sensor data, such as the presence of shadows, rain or fog, and still make correct decisions. If a model is not robust, it can easily be thrown off balance by such disturbances, which can lead to dangerous maneuvers such as abrupt braking or swerving. This not only endangers the occupants of the vehicle, but also other road users.

Another example of the importance of robustness is medical diagnostics. In this field, AI systems need to make accurate and reliable diagnoses, often based on different and sometimes incomplete medical data. A robust model can deal with varying data quality and still provide accurate diagnoses. If a model is not robust, it may make incorrect diagnoses when confronted with incomplete or slightly erroneous data. This can have serious consequences for patients, including incorrect treatments and delayed recovery processes.

The robustness of AI systems also plays a decisive role in the financial sector. Financial markets are dynamic and influenced by many unpredictable factors. A robust model can make stable predictions and decisions under different market conditions, which is crucial for the success and reliability of financial strategies. A non-robust model could be overwhelmed by unexpected market changes, which can lead to significant financial losses.

The robustness of AI systems is also crucial for the trustworthiness and acceptance of such systems. If users know that an AI system delivers reliable results even under varying conditions, trust in the technology increases. This is particularly important in safety-critical applications, where the consequences of misconduct can be severe. A robust system signals to users that it will work reliably even in unexpected situations, which promotes acceptance and trust in the technology.

The development of robust AI systems requires careful modeling and validation. This includes the use of diverse and representative training data that reflects the diversity and complexity of the real world. By integrating data augmentation techniques, models can be made more robust to variations in the input data. Regularization techniques help to control the complexity of the model and avoid overfitting, which improves the generalization capability of the model.

Another important aspect of robustness is the continuous monitoring and maintenance of the models once they have been deployed. The environments in which AI systems are deployed can change over time, and new data can bring new challenges. Regular updates and adjustments to the models are necessary to ensure that they continue to work robustly and reliably. This includes implementing mechanisms to detect and correct misbehavior as well as adapting the models to new data and conditions.

Robustness can also be improved by using ensembling methods, where multiple models are combined to stabilize the overall performance. These methods utilize the strengths of different models and reduce the likelihood of a single model failing due to variations in the data. Ensembling can help to increase the reliability and stability of predictions and reduce the susceptibility to incorrect inputs.

Consequences and risks of psychotic AI

Effects on decisions and systems

One of the most serious consequences of "AI psychosis" is the loss of trust in the technology. When AI models make faulty decisions or show bias, users and organizations lose trust in the systems. This can lead to lower acceptance and use of AI technologies and significantly impair their benefits and efficiency. Such mistrust can affect all areas where AI is used, from medicine to finance to criminal justice.

Social inequalities can be reinforced by the bias of AI systems. When algorithms are trained on biased data, they perpetuate existing discrimination and injustice. Similar risks exist in other areas such as human resources, lending and healthcare, where biased algorithms can negatively impact the opportunities and quality of life of disadvantaged groups.

Another challenge with AI systems is the lack of transparency and accountability. Many AI models, especially those based on deep learning, are complex and difficult to interpret. This "black box" nature of the models makes it difficult to understand decisions and assign responsibilities. In the event of wrong decisions, it is often difficult to determine who can be held responsible, making legal and ethical oversight of the technology considerably more difficult.

In addition, AI psychoses can pose direct safety risks. In safety-critical applications such as autonomous driving or medical diagnosis, poor decisions can lead to physical harm or even loss of life. This underlines the need for strict safety and testing protocols for AI systems to ensure that they operate reliably and safely in critical situations.

The impact of AI psychosis on corporate decision-making is also significant. Organizations using AI for decision making need to consider the risks of AI psychosis, as poor decisions can have significant financial and reputational consequences. Many companies are therefore investing in robust validation and monitoring mechanisms to ensure the integrity of their AI models and minimize the risk of poor decisions.

At a regulatory and ethical level, the challenges posed by AI psychosis have already led to the development of stricter framework conditions. Governments and international organizations are working on guidelines to ensure the transparency, fairness and safety of AI systems. These measures also include requirements for the documentation and explanation of decision-making processes by AI to ensure that the systems operate in a traceable and responsible manner.

Wrong decisions in sensitive areas (e.g. justice, medicine)

Erroneous decisions in sensitive areas such as justice and medicine caused by erratic AI phenomena are particularly worrying. The so-called psychoses of AI - the erroneous or biased decisions made by AI systems - have the potential to significantly undermine trust in these technologies and have serious consequences for the individuals concerned and society as a whole.

In the justice system, the use of AI systems to predict recidivism probabilities or to assist in making decisions about bail denials and sentencing can have a profound impact. Algorithms trained on historical data often reflect the biases and inequities present in that data. This can lead to certain population groups, particularly minorities, being systematically disadvantaged. For example, if an AI system indicates a higher likelihood for members of certain ethnic groups when predicting the likelihood of recidivism, based on historical arrest and conviction data, it perpetuates existing inequalities in the criminal justice system. This can lead to harsher sentences and longer prison terms for these groups, further increasing social injustice and undermining trust in the legal system.

In the medical field, the mistakes made by AI systems can be just as devastating. AI is increasingly being used to diagnose diseases, predict disease progression and assist with treatment decisions. However, if the underlying data on which these systems have been trained contains biases or inaccuracies, the resulting diagnoses and recommendations can be equally flawed. An example would be an AI system that is less likely to interpret certain symptoms in women or ethnic minorities as indicators of serious illness due to incomplete or biased data. This can lead to serious conditions being overlooked or misdiagnosed, resulting in inadequate or incorrect treatment. The health consequences for patients can be serious, including exacerbation of illness or even death if life-saving treatments are not administered in a timely manner.

These wrong decisions are exacerbated by the "black box" nature of many AI models. The complexity and opacity of the algorithms often make it difficult to understand the reasons for certain decisions. In the justice system, this can mean that a defendant or their defense cannot understand why a particular risk score has led to a harsher sentence. In medicine, doctors and patients may not be able to understand why a particular diagnosis was made or treatment recommended, further undermining trust in the healthcare system.

Furthermore, these wrong decisions pose ethical and legal challenges. Who bears responsibility if an AI-supported decision is demonstrably wrong and leads to an unjust judgment or an incorrect medical diagnosis? Assigning responsibility becomes particularly difficult when decision-making is based on complex algorithms developed and implemented by different actors. This requires careful consideration of ethical principles and the creation of clear regulatory frameworks to ensure that AI systems are transparent and accountable.

Potential economic damage

The potential economic damage caused by wrong decisions and bias can also be considerable.

One significant risk is that incorrect decisions made by AI systems in companies can lead to considerable financial losses. For example, if an AI system is used in the financial sector to make trading decisions, incorrect analysis or bias in the underlying data can lead to suboptimal investment decisions. This can lead to significant financial losses for companies and investors. Similarly, AI-powered credit scoring models that contain biases can lead to incorrect loan default predictions, affecting lending practices and increasing the risk of loan defaults.

In addition, wrong decisions in supply chain and logistics planning based on incorrect AI analyses can cause considerable economic damage. If an AI system makes incorrect forecasts about demand or delivery times, this can lead to inefficient warehouse management, overstocking or supply bottlenecks. This not only directly affects the companies concerned, but can also lead to disruptions in the entire supply chain, affecting economic activity in various industries.

The lack of transparency and explainability of many AI models exacerbates these problems. If companies do not fully understand the decision-making processes of their AI systems, they are less able to recognize and correct potential errors. This can lead to a chain reaction of bad decisions that have a negative impact on overall economic performance.

Legal and regulatory consequences can also result in significant economic damage. If companies violate legal regulations or ethical standards due to incorrect AI decisions, they can face high fines and claims for damages. This is particularly relevant in highly regulated industries such as the financial sector, healthcare and data protection. Such legal consequences can not only cause immediate financial damage, but can also permanently damage a company's reputation and undermine the trust of customers and investors.

In addition, the introduction of flawed or biased AI systems can lead to a loss of consumer trust. If customers feel that they are being treated unfairly by AI decisions, be it credit decisions, insurance claims or personalized services, this can lead to customer churn and a decline in sales. Companies must therefore ensure that their AI systems are fair, transparent and reliable in order to gain and maintain customer trust.

In the long term, the economic damage caused by "AI psychosis" can also affect the innovative strength and competitiveness of companies and entire industries. If companies are reluctant to use or further develop AI technologies because they fear the potential risks, this can affect technological progress and competitiveness on a global scale. This is particularly relevant at a time when technological innovation is a driving force for economic growth and development.

Social acceptance of AI

The social acceptance of artificial intelligence is a difficult issue that is influenced by various factors. These include trust in the technology, the perceived fairness and ethics of the applications, as well as the transparency and explainability of the decision-making processes. In order to promote the acceptance of AI in society, these factors must be carefully addressed.

First of all, trust plays a decisive role. The broad acceptance of AI depends largely on how trustworthy the technology is perceived to be. Trust is created through transparent processes, comprehensible decision-making paths and reliable performance. When AI systems are able to deliver consistent and correct results, user trust increases. This is particularly important in critical areas such as healthcare, justice and finance, where wrong decisions can have serious consequences. A trustworthy AI system must be comprehensible so that users can understand how and why certain decisions are made. This explainability helps to strengthen trust and promote acceptance.

Another important factor is the perception of the fairness and ethics of AI applications. Social acceptance depends heavily on whether people believe that AI acts fairly and without bias. Historical prejudice and discrimination embedded in training data can lead to biased decisions that systematically disadvantage certain groups. This can significantly undermine trust in the technology. To avoid this, developers must ensure that

AI systems are trained on diverse and representative data sets. In addition, mechanisms to detect and mitigate bias should be implemented to ensure fair and equitable decisions.

The transparency and explainability of AI systems are also crucial for their social acceptance. People must be able to understand the decision-making processes of AI in order to develop trust in the technology. This requires not only technical solutions, but also clear communication strategies that explain how AI works in an understandable way. Education and information play a central role here. Targeted educational programs can reduce misunderstandings and fears and create a better understanding of the possibilities and limitations of AI. An informed public is more willing to accept and support AI applications.

The ethical implications of using AI must also be carefully considered. This includes compliance with data protection regulations and the responsible handling of personal data. Society must ensure that the use of AI is in line with ethical norms and values. This can be achieved through the development and implementation of ethical guidelines and standards that promote the responsible use of AI. Regulatory authorities and policy makers have an important role to play here by creating frameworks that ensure the ethical use of AI.

Another element that influences the social acceptance of AI is the integration of the technology into everyday life. The more people have positive experiences with AI applications, the more likely they are to accept the technology. This can be supported by user-friendly designs and intuitive interfaces that make it easier for people to interact with AI systems. Successful applications in areas such as voice assistants, personalized recommendations and automated services can help increase adoption by demonstrating the benefits and advantages of AI in everyday life.

Finally, public perception and media coverage play an important role in the social acceptance of AI. Sensational reporting on the potential dangers and misuse of AI can fuel fears and reduce acceptance.

Trust in AI systems

Trust in AI systems is a key issue, especially in the context of so-called "psychoses of AI". These psychoses, which can be described as flawed or biased decisions made by AI systems, have the potential to significantly undermine trust in these technologies.

First of all, the transparency of AI systems is a key factor for trust. Transparency means that the AI's decision-making processes are comprehensible and understandable. This is particularly important when it comes to complex algorithms that are based on deep learning.

Another critical aspect is the fairness of AI systems. Trust will only arise if people can be sure that the AI's decisions are fair and unbiased. The challenge is that AI systems are trained on historical data that may contain biases and prejudices. These biases can be embedded in the models and then reproduced in the AI's decisions. To address this issue, developers need to ensure that the training data is representative and balanced. In addition, algorithms should be used to detect and correct biases. Techniques such as "bias mitigation" and "fairness constraints" can help to improve the fairness of AI systems and thus increase user confidence.

The reliability and robustness of AI systems are also crucial for trust. Users must be able to trust that the AI will make consistent and correct decisions under different conditions. This requires extensive testing and validation of the models to ensure that they work reliably in practice. A robust AI must be able to deal with unexpected inputs and situations without making incorrect or dangerous decisions.

Another key element is the ethical design and use of AI. Trust will only be built if people can be sure that the technology is being used in accordance with ethical standards. This includes the protection of privacy and the responsible handling of personal data. In addition, ethical guidelines should be developed and implemented to promote the responsible use of AI. These guidelines should address issues of fairness, transparency and accountability and ensure that the technology is used for the benefit of society.

Importance of trust for acceptance

Trust plays a central role in the acceptance of artificial intelligence in society. Without trust in the technology, its processes and results, it is unlikely that people and organizations will use AI systems on a large scale. The importance of trust for the acceptance of AI can be seen in several important aspects.

First of all, trust is key to overcoming skepticism and resistance to new technologies. Artificial intelligence, especially advanced forms such as machine learning and neural networks, can seem scary or opaque to many people. If people feel that they do not understand how AI works and the decision-making processes involved, they tend to distrust and reject these technologies. Trust comes from transparency and traceability, which help users understand the mechanisms behind AI. When users see that the technology is transparent and explainable, they are more willing to accept and use it.

Another important element is the perception of the reliability and accuracy of AI systems. In critical applications, such as medical diagnosis or autonomous vehicle control, trust in the accuracy and reliability of AI is crucial. Faulty or inaccurate decisions can not only lead to significant financial losses, but also endanger human lives. If users can trust that AI systems are accurate and reliable, they will be more willing to accept these technologies and use them in important areas.

Fairness and ethics are also of great importance for the trust and acceptance of AI. Societies are increasingly concerned about the ethical implications of AI, particularly in relation to bias and discrimination. If AI systems are perceived as unfair or biased, this undermines user trust and can lead to widespread rejection of the technology. AI developers and providers need to ensure that their systems operate in a fair and unbiased manner by using diverse and representative data sets and implementing bias mitigation mechanisms. Ethical guidelines and standards are also required to ensure that AI systems are operated in accordance with society's moral values.

Trust also encourages innovation and a willingness to try out new technologies. When people and organizations have confidence in the safety and reliability of AI, they are more willing to invest in these technologies and test them in different areas. This can lead to a faster spread and acceptance of AI and at the same time strengthen the innovative power and competitiveness of companies and countries.

Furthermore, trust plays an essential role in the social integration and long-term acceptance of AI. In an increasingly digitalized world in which AI is playing an ever greater role, it is important that all parts of society have access to and trust in these technologies. This requires targeted education and awareness-raising work to promote understanding and trust in AI. A well-informed and educated public is more likely to take advantage of AI and fully exploit its potential.

Consequences of loss of trust

A loss of trust in artificial intelligence can have far-reaching consequences that extend to various levels of society and the economy.

First of all, a loss of trust leads to less acceptance and use of AI technologies. Companies may be reluctant to invest in AI or use it in critical areas such as healthcare, finance or criminal justice. Another significant aspect is the economic damage that can result from a loss of trust. Companies that rely heavily on AI can suffer significant financial losses if their customers or partners lose trust in their systems. In the public perception, a loss of trust in AI can also lead to broader skepticism towards technological innovation. If the public loses trust in AI, this can result in a general reluctance to embrace new technologies and innovations. This skepticism can have a negative impact on the willingness to accept and use new technologies, which can inhibit overall technological progress.

Furthermore, a loss of trust in AI systems can affect innovation and research progress in this area. If researchers and developers feel that their work is not widely accepted or supported, this could reduce motivation and engagement in AI research. Another significant aspect is the ethical and social dimension of a loss of trust in AI. If AI systems are perceived as unfair or discriminatory, this can exacerbate social tensions and inequalities. The perception that certain groups or individuals are systematically disadvantaged can undermine social trust in technological and institutional systems. This could lead to increased polarization and a loss of social cohesion, which could have serious social and political consequences.

Strategies for prevention and control

Data validation and cleansing

The prevention and control of incorrect decisions using artificial intelligence requires, above all, careful data validation and cleansing.

The foundation of any AI application is the quality of the data on which the algorithms are trained. Data validation and cleansing are therefore essential to ensure that the data sets are free of errors, distortions and anomalies.

This begins with a thorough check of the raw data. The data must be checked for completeness and consistency. Missing or inconsistent data can lead to incorrect conclusions and affect the performance of the AI system. A thorough validation process ensures that all relevant data is correctly recorded and documented.

Cleansing the data is the next critical step. This involves identifying and removing incorrect, irrelevant or duplicate data. This process helps to improve the accuracy and quality of the data set. An example of this would be the removal of outliers or data points that are clearly outside the normal range and could distort the analysis. In addition, it is important that the data representation is balanced. An uneven data set that over-represents or under-represents certain groups or characteristics can lead to a biased AI model. The cleansing should therefore ensure that the data is diverse and representative to promote fair and balanced decisions.

Another aspect of data validation and cleansing is checking for bias and systematic distortions. Historical data often contains unconscious biases that can be embedded in AI models. These biases can have a negative impact on decision-making and systematically disadvantage certain groups. To prevent this, the data must be checked for various types of bias, such as gender, race or age bias. Techniques such as fairness checks and bias mitigation strategies can help to identify and correct these biases. Continuous monitoring of data and models is necessary to ensure that new biases are not introduced.

Data enrichment is a complementary process to validation and cleansing, in which additional relevant information is integrated into the data set to improve the analysis. This can be done, for example, by adding external data sources or by applying data augmentation techniques. A richer and more diverse database can increase the robustness and accuracy of the AI model and help to minimize wrong decisions.

An important step in the prevention and control of incorrect AI decisions is also the documentation and transparency of data processes. Clear and detailed documentation of the data sources, the cleansing and validation techniques used and the assumptions and decisions made is crucial. This transparency makes it possible to understand and review the data quality and decision-making processes of the AI system. It is also important for accountability and compliance with legal and ethical standards.

Techniques to avoid overfitting

Overfitting, or overfitting a model to the training data, is another common problem in machine learning that can significantly affect the generalization ability of a model. To avoid overfitting and ensure that a model performs well on new, unknown data, there are a variety of techniques that can be applied. These techniques range from improving data quality and variety to specific adjustments in the model architecture and training process.

One of the most basic techniques to avoid overfitting is to use more training data. When a model is trained on a larger and more diverse set of data, it has a better chance of learning the underlying patterns and not just the noise and randomness in the data. However, collecting and curating additional data can be expensive and time consuming, so it is often necessary to use other techniques to get the best out of the available data.

Another approach is data augmentation, particularly in image processing. Data augmentation involves generating new training examples by applying various transformations to existing data, such as rotating, scaling, flipping and distorting images. This technique effectively increases the size of the training dataset and helps the model to become more robust to variations in the data. This reduces the likelihood of the model learning specific details of the training data that are not relevant for generalization.

Regularization is a widely used technique to avoid overfitting, which consists of introducing additional constraints or penalties on the model parameters during training. L1 and L2 regularization are two common forms of regularization. L1 regularization adds a penalty to the absolute sum of the model weights, resulting in some weights being set to zero and thus making the model more parsimonious. L2 regularization adds a penalty for the squared sum of the model weights, which keeps the weights smaller overall and reduces the complexity of the model. Both techniques help to constrain the capacity of the model and reduce the risk of overfitting.

Dropout is a specific technique used in deep neural networks to avoid overfitting. In dropout, randomly selected neurons are deactivated during training, which prevents the model from becoming too dependent on certain paths and connections. This forces the model to learn more redundant and robust features that generalize better. Dropout reduces the model's dependence on specific neurons and connections and helps improve generalization ability.

Cross-validation is another important technique that helps to evaluate model performance and avoid overfitting. In cross-validation, the training dataset is divided into several parts, and the model is trained and validated multiple times by using one part at a time as the validation set and the remaining parts as the training set. This helps to better assess and improve the generalization ability of the model as the model is tested on different subsets of the data. It provides a more robust estimate of model performance and helps to reduce the risk of overfitting.

Another method to avoid overfitting is to use a validation dataset and an early stop during the training process. A validation dataset, which is not used for training, is used to monitor the model performance. With the early stop, the training process is aborted if the performance on the validation dataset no longer improves or deteriorates. This prevents the model from being trained for too long and starting to learn the noise in the training data.

Ensembling methods, such as bagging and boosting, are also effective techniques for avoiding overfitting. In bagging (bootstrap aggregating), several models are trained on different subsets of the data and their predictions are combined. This reduces the variance and helps to achieve more robust predictions. Random forests are a popular example of bagging. Boosting methods, such as gradient boosting, sequentially train multiple models, with each new model aiming to correct the errors of the previous models. This leads to a strong reduction in bias and variance, which improves generalization ability.

Careful selection of model architecture and hyperparameters is also crucial to avoid overfitting. More complex models are more prone to overfitting, especially when trained on small or insufficient datasets. By using simpler models and optimizing the hyperparameters, such as learning rate, number of layers and neurons, the risk of overfitting can be reduced. Hyperparameter optimization techniques, such as grid search or random search, can help to find the best settings that provide a good balance between model complexity and generalization ability.

Robustness in modeling

Lack of robustness in modeling is another significant cause of the phenomenon of "psychosis" in AI systems, where the behavior of the AI appears unpredictable, irrational or illogical. Robustness in modeling refers to the ability of a model to perform reliably and consistently under various conditions, including when confronted with unexpected inputs, noise or other disturbances. If a model is not robust, it can easily become unbalanced and produce erroneous or absurd results.

One of the main causes of a lack of robustness is a model's inability to generalize to new or unusual inputs. Models that have only been trained on a narrow set of training data may learn specific patterns and features of that data instead of deriving general and robust rules. If the model is then confronted with new or different data that is not well represented by the training data, it may fail or produce unexpected results. For example, a language assistant trained primarily on formal text may have difficulty understanding and processing informal or dialectal speech, resulting in confusing or inappropriate responses.

Another factor that contributes to the lack of robustness is overfitting (see above). If a model is overfitted to the training data, it learns not only the relevant patterns, but also the noise and randomness in the data. This leads to the model generalizing poorly on new data that does not contain these specific details. Overfitting can be exacerbated by the complexity of the model. Complex models with many parameters have a high capacity to capture the details of the training data, but are also more prone to overfitting and therefore less robust to new data.

Another aspect of the lack of robustness in modeling is sensitivity to noise or small changes in the input data. Robust models should be able to deal with minor deviations or disturbances without significantly affecting their performance. However, if a model is very sensitive to such changes, this can lead to unstable and unpredictable results. An example of this is image processing, where small changes in pixel values, such as those caused by noise or image processing, can cause an image classification model to make incorrect or absurd predictions.

The architecture and design of the model also play a crucial role in robustness. Models that have not been carefully designed and validated are more prone to errors and instabilities. For example, neural networks with a suboptimal architecture may tend to find local minima in the error landscape, leading to suboptimal solutions and a lack of robustness. Choosing the right model architecture and using techniques such as regularization and cross-validation are crucial to ensure the robustness of the model.

Another important factor is data quality and diversity. Models that are trained on high quality and diverse data tend to be more robust and able to generalize to a wide range of scenarios. The lack of robustness can also be exacerbated by insufficient testing and validation during the development phase. Models should be thoroughly tested on different data sets and under different conditions to assess their robustness and generalizability. If these tests are not performed adequately, the model may produce unexpected and unpredictable results in practice.

The implementation of techniques to increase robustness is crucial to minimize the risk of "psychosis" in AI systems. One such technique is data augmentation, where the training data is augmented by various transformations to make the model more robust to variations in the inputs. Dropout and other regularization methods can also be used to reduce overfitting and increase robustness. In addition, ensembling methods that combine multiple models can improve the robustness and reliability of predictions.

Another important approach is the continuous monitoring and adaptation of models after deployment. Models deployed in the real world should be regularly monitored and reviewed to ensure that they continue to operate robustly and reliably. This includes adapting the models to new data and conditions as well as implementing mechanisms to detect and correct misbehavior.

Bias checks and regular monitoring

Ensuring that bias is minimized is a crucial aspect in the development and implementation of artificial intelligence.

Bias checks begin with careful analysis and evaluation of the data sets used to train AI models. Historical data can reflect inherent biases and inequalities that, if left undetected, can become embedded in AI models and influence their decisions. An important step is to analyze the distribution of data across different demographic groups and ensure that no group is over- or under-represented. This can be done through statistical analysis and visualizations that highlight potential biases in the data.

The use of specific metrics to assess bias is also critical. These metrics include statistical methods such as the disparate impact ratio, which examines whether a model's results are the same for different groups, and analyzing false positive and false negative rates to identify differences in misclassification. By using such metrics, developers can identify potential biases in the models and assess how much these biases affect different demographic groups.

Another key approach to minimizing bias is the use of fairness algorithms and bias mitigation techniques. These techniques can be applied before, during and after the training of models. Before training, methods such as reweighting or resampling can be used to ensure that the training data is balanced. During training, fairness constraints can be integrated into the optimization processes to ensure that the models make fair decisions. After training, techniques such as post-processing can be applied to check and adjust the model's decisions to reduce bias.

Regular monitoring is also crucial to ensure that the models continue to operate fairly and reliably. An important part of regular monitoring is the performance of audits and reviews. These audits should be conducted regularly and systematically to verify compliance with established fairness and quality standards. Independent reviews by external experts can provide additional security and help to ensure that the models comply with ethical and legal requirements. The involvement of domain experts and stakeholders in the monitoring process is also crucial. These experts bring valuable knowledge and perspectives that can help to identify and address potential biases. Through regular consultations and feedback rounds with stakeholders, developers can ensure that models meet practical requirements and ethical standards. This promotes continuous improvement of the models and supports the long-term acceptance and trustworthiness of the AI systems.

In addition to technical monitoring, organizational measures should also be taken to promote a culture of fairness and accountability. This includes training employees on bias detection and fairness practices, establishing clear guidelines and standards for model development and monitoring, and creating mechanisms for reporting and addressing concerns and issues related to bias. Strong organizational support and a shared commitment to ethical AI practices are critical to achieving long-term success in minimizing bias and ensuring data quality.

Techniques for identifying and correcting bias

Some of the most important techniques for identifying and correcting bias are described in detail below.

Identification of bias

Descriptive statistics and visualization

A basic method for identifying bias is the use of descriptive statistics and visualization techniques. By analyzing the distribution of data characteristics such as gender, age, ethnicity and other demographic characteristics, imbalances and biases in the data sets can be identified. Histograms, boxplots and scatterplots are helpful tools for visualizing possible bias patterns.

Disparate Impact Analysis

The Disparate Impact Analysis assesses whether a decision or prediction of a model has different effects on different groups. This analysis uses statistical metrics such as the disparate impact ratio, which measures the ratio of positive outcomes for a protected group compared to a reference group. A significant difference in results indicates potential bias.

Analysis of false positives/false negatives

Another means of identifying bias is to analyze the misclassification rates (false positives and false negatives) for different groups. Differences in these rates can indicate systematic biases in the model. For example, a higher proportion of false positives for a particular demographic group could indicate a bias in the model.

Correction of bias

Pre-processing techniques

Pre-processing techniques aim to correct biases in the data before training the model. These include methods such as:

Reweighting

Reweighting is a technique in machine learning and data processing that aims to achieve a more balanced distribution of different groups within a data set. This method is often used to correct biases in data and ensure that machine learning models make fair and just predictions.

Reweighting refers to the process of adjusting the weights of individual data points in a dataset to achieve a more representative and balanced distribution of group characteristics. This means that data points from underrepresented groups are given a higher weight, while data points from overrepresented groups are given a lower weight. The aim is to minimize distortions caused by unequal group sizes and to enable the learning algorithms to develop fairer models.

The technical implementation of reweighting takes place in several steps. First, the data set is analyzed to understand the distribution of the different groups. This includes identifying the group characteristics (such as gender, ethnicity, age, etc.) and quantifying their frequency in the data set. Based on this analysis, the weightings of the data points are adjusted. This can be done using various methods, such as inverse frequency or Bayesian weighting.

A commonly used approach is inverse frequency weighting, where the weighting of a data point is inversely proportional to the frequency of its group in the data set. For example, if one group makes up only 10% of the dataset while another group makes up 90%, the data points of the smaller group are given a weighting that is nine times higher than that of the larger group. This forces the model to take greater account of the smaller group when building the model.

The implementation of reweighting brings with it a number of challenges. One of the biggest challenges is finding the right balance. Overweighting underrepresented groups can lead to overfitting, where the model reacts disproportionately to the few data points from these groups. Underweighting, on the other hand, may not sufficiently correct for bias.

Another important aspect is data quality. If the data points from the underrepresented groups are of poorer quality or have systematic errors, reweighting can exacerbate these problems instead of solving them. Therefore, careful data preparation and analysis is crucial before reweighting is applied.

Reweighting is used in many areas where fair and balanced models are needed. In health research, for example, it can be used to ensure that medical models are not only based on data from one demographic group, but also take other groups into account appropriately. This is particularly important in areas where there are historical inequalities in data availability.

Another example is the use of reweighting in credit assessment. Here, the technique can help to ensure that models are fair to different ethnic groups or genders by ensuring that no group is disadvantaged due to unequal data distributions.

Resampling

Resampling is a widely used technique in machine learning and data processing that aims to achieve a more balanced distribution of groups within a dataset. This method is particularly useful for correcting biases and imbalances that arise when certain groups are underrepresented or overrepresented in the training data. Resampling can be used to develop models that make fairer and more accurate predictions.

Resampling comprises two main approaches: Oversampling and Undersampling. Oversampling refers to the duplication of data points from underrepresented groups to increase their number in the dataset. This is done to ensure that the model receives enough examples from these groups to better learn their characteristics. Undersampling, on the other hand, involves removing data points from overrepresented groups to reduce their number. This prevents the model from being too fixated on the more frequent groups and neglecting the rarer groups.

The main goal of resampling is to create a balance in the training data so that all groups are equally well represented in the data set. This ensures that the model does not develop systematic biases and makes fair predictions for all groups.

The implementation of resampling requires a careful analysis of the distribution of the different groups in the data set. First, the data set is examined for imbalances by determining the frequencies of the various group characteristics. Based on this analysis, a decision is made as to which groups need to be oversampled or undersampled. Oversampling can be carried out in various ways. A simple approach is to randomly duplicate data points from the underrepresented groups. A more advanced method is to synthetically generate new data points using techniques such as the Synthetic Minority Over-sampling Technique (SMOTE). SMOTE creates new data points by combining and varying the characteristics of existing data points. Undersampling can be achieved by randomly removing data points from the over-represented groups. A less risky method is to select the data points in such a way that the variance within the groups is preserved. This can be done by stratified sampling, where the most important characteristics of the data points are taken into account.

The application of resampling brings with it various challenges. When oversampling, there is a risk of overfitting, as the model may react too strongly to the duplicated data points, making it less generalizable. With undersampling, there is a risk of information loss as important data points may be removed, which can limit the model's ability to recognize patterns in the data. Another important aspect is data quality. If the underrepresented groups inherently contain noisier or less representative data, resampling can exacerbate these problems rather than solve them. Therefore, careful pre-processing of the data and thorough analysis of group characteristics is essential.

Resampling is used in many areas where it is crucial to develop fair and accurate models. A prominent example is medical research, where the distribution of patient groups is often unbalanced. Resampling can ensure that the model can reliably make predictions for all patient groups, regardless of gender, age or ethnicity. Another example is fraud detection in financial transactions. Fraud cases are usually rare, so the data is highly imbalanced. By oversampling the fraud cases, a model can be better trained to recognize these rare events without being dominated by the overwhelming majority of non-fraudulent cases.

Resampling is an essential technique for correcting imbalances in data sets and promoting fairness in machine learning models. By selectively over- or under-matching data points, a balance in the training data is achieved, leading to fairer and more representative models. Despite the challenges associated with the implementation of resampling, this method offers an effective way to improve the quality and fairness of predictive models and ensure ethical standards in data processing.

Data Augmentation

Data augmentation is a technique used in machine learning and data processing to supplement existing data sets with synthetically generated data points. The aim of this method is to increase the diversity and representativeness of the data, thereby improving the performance of models and avoiding overfitting. This technique is particularly useful in areas such as image and speech recognition and natural language processing, where the availability of large and diverse datasets is crucial.

Data augmentation works by applying various transformations to existing data points to create new, slightly varied versions of that data. In image processing, such transformations can include rotating, scaling, flipping, cropping or adding noise to images. These techniques simulate real-world variations that make the model robust to similar, but not identical, patterns during training.

An example of the application of data augmentation in image processing would be the use of a training data set of cat images. Through transformations such as rotating the images by different angles, changing the brightness or adding noise, the dataset can be artificially augmented. This helps the model to generalize better by training it on a wider variety of appearances, improving the overall recognition ability for cat images.

In natural language processing, data augmentation can be achieved through techniques such as synonym replacement, random word deletion or adding noise to text. For example, a sentence such as "The weather is beautiful today" could be changed to "The weather is beautiful today" by replacing "beautiful" with "glorious". These variations help the model to learn a more robust representation of the language and improve its ability to deal with new and unpredictable formulations.

Another area in which data augmentation plays an important role is speech recognition. Here, synthetically generated audio data can be created by adding background noise, changing the speed of speech or modifying the pitch. These augmented data points help to increase the diversity of the training data set, leading to better recognition and interpretation of spoken words and sentences.

Although data augmentation offers many benefits, there are also challenges and limitations. One of the challenges is to ensure that the augmented data points retain the underlying characteristics and patterns of the original data and do not lead to a degradation in model performance. If the applied transformations are too extreme or introduce irrelevant variations, this can confuse the model and impair its ability to generalize.

Another potential problem is the computational intensity of data augmentation. Creating and processing a large number of synthetic data points can require significant computational resources, which in some cases can increase the training time and infrastructure required. Therefore, it is important to develop efficient algorithms and techniques to effectively implement data augmentation without overburdening resources.

In-processing techniques

In-processing techniques are used during the training of the model to minimize bias. These include:

Fairness constraints

Fairness constraints are an important technique in machine learning that aims to integrate fairness constraints directly into the training process of models. The goal of this technique is to ensure that the models make fair decisions and avoid systematic bias and discrimination. This is often achieved by modifying the loss function to optimize both prediction accuracy and fairness.

The implementation of fairness constraints begins with the definition of specific fairness criteria that are to be taken into account in the model. These criteria can vary depending on the use case, but often include aspects such as demographic parity, equalized odds or equal chances. Demographic parity requires that the prediction results for different demographic groups are similarly distributed. Equalized odds ensures that the false-positive and false-negative rates are the same for all groups. Equal odds means that the probability of a correct positive prediction is the same for all groups.

Once the fairness criteria have been defined, the model's loss function is modified. The loss function is a mathematical construct that measures the performance of the model and defines the goal of the training process. By adding fairness conditions to the loss function, the model is forced to optimize both the prediction accuracy and the fulfillment of the fairness criteria. This can be achieved by introducing additional terms into the loss function that quantify and penalize the deviation from the fairness targets.

An example of a modified loss function could look like this: Suppose we have a standard loss function $L(y, \hat{y})$ that measures the discrepancy between the actual values y and the predicted values $\hat{y}$

\). To integrate fairness, we could add an additional term F that represents the fairness condition. The modified loss function could then be $L(y, \hat{y}) + \lambda F$, where λ is a hyperparameter that determines the relative weight of the fairness condition. By adjusting λ, the model can balance between prediction accuracy and fairness.

The introduction of fairness constraints into the training process brings with it several challenges. One of the biggest challenges is finding the right balance between fairness and accuracy. Too much focus on fairness can reduce the overall accuracy of the model, while too much focus on accuracy can neglect fairness. It requires careful tuning and validation to ensure that the model achieves both goals to an appropriate degree.

Another problem is the complexity of the fairness criteria themselves. Different fairness criteria can conflict with each other and it is often difficult to find a solution that fulfills all criteria at the same time. In addition, fairness criteria can vary depending on context and application, which means that the implementation of fairness constraints must be tailored and adapted to specific requirements.

A practical example of the application of fairness constraints is the development of a credit scoring model that ensures that no demographic group is disadvantaged due to their ethnicity or gender. By integrating fairness constraints into the model's loss function, it can be ensured that the model makes fair credit decisions by ensuring the same probability of credit approvals for all groups.

Adversarial debiasing

Adversarial debiasing is an innovative technique in the field of machine learning that aims to reduce bias in models. This method uses adversarial networks to detect and eliminate systematic biases while continuing to train the main model to make accurate predictions. This approach represents a combination of the strength of adversarial networks and the need for fair decision making.

The basic concept of adversarial networks was originally introduced in the context of generative adversarial networks (GANs), where two networks play against each other: a generator that tries to produce realistic data and a discriminator that tries to distinguish real from generated data. Adversarial debiasing adapts this principle to combat biases in the data and the models.

In adversarial debiasing, the setup consists of two main components: the prediction model and the adversarial network. As usual, the prediction model is trained to make accurate predictions for the target variable. In parallel, the adversarial network is trained to recognize biases in the model's predictions. The training process is designed so that the prediction model learns to make predictions that are both accurate and free of bias in order to fool the adversarial network.

The training process begins by training the prediction model on the original data to make accurate predictions. During this training, the predictions of the model and the true labels are fed as inputs to the adversarial network. The adversarial network is trained to recognize whether the model's predictions contain bias based on the demographic characteristics of the data.

To reduce the bias, a feedback mechanism is implemented. If the adversarial network detects bias in the predictions, a feedback signal is sent to the prediction model. This feedback signal is used to adjust the weights of the prediction model so that future predictions contain less bias. The aim is to train the prediction model so that it not only makes accurate predictions, but also predictions that the adversarial network cannot recognize as biased.

A practical example of adversarial debiasing is the development of a recruitment model that evaluates job applications. The prediction model is trained to assess the suitability of applicants based on their qualifications. At the same time, the adversarial network is trained to recognize whether the predictions of the model are influenced by demographic characteristics such as gender or ethnicity. Through the iterative training process, the prediction model learns to make predictions that are free of these biases, resulting in fairer hiring decisions.

However, the application of adversarial debiasing also brings challenges. One of the biggest challenges is finding the balance between accuracy and fairness. Too much focus on removing bias can reduce the overall accuracy of the model. Another aspect is the complexity of implementation. The training process requires careful coordination of the two networks, which requires additional computational resources and expertise.

Post-processing techniques

Post-processing techniques are used after training the model to correct biases in the predictions.

Equalized Odds

Equalized odds is an important method in the field of fairness in machine learning that aims to adjust the predictions of a model so that the false-positive and false-negative rates are the same for different demographic groups. This concept ensures that the model has similar error probabilities regardless of the group to which the data points belong and therefore does not systematically disadvantage or favor individual groups.

The core idea of Equalized Odds is to ensure the equality of error rates between different groups. Mathematically, this means that the probability that the model makes a positive prediction, given that the actual outcome is positive (true positive rate), and the probability that the model makes a negative prediction, given that the actual outcome is negative (true negative rate), should be the same for all groups. Formally, the conditions for Equalized Odds are as follows:

$P(\hat{Y} = 1 \mid Y = 1, A = a) = P(\hat{Y} = 1 \mid Y = 1, A = b)$ for all groups a and b,

$P(\hat{Y} = 0 \mid Y = 0, A = a) = P(\hat{Y} = 0 \mid Y = 0, A = b)$ for all groups a and b.

Here $\hat{Y}$ stands for the prediction of the model, Y for the actual result and A for the demographic group.

The implementation of Equalized Odds in a model training requires specific adjustments to ensure that the error rates are equalized for all groups. One way to achieve this is to adjust the model afterwards or to apply specific optimization techniques during the training process. A commonly used method is to modify the loss function of the model to optimize not only the prediction accuracy but also the compliance with the equalized odds. This can be done by introducing additional fairness terms into the loss function that minimize the deviations of the error rates between the groups.

A practical example of the application of Equalized Odds is the development of a credit scoring model that ensures that the false positive and false negative rates are equal for different ethnic groups. Without adjustments, certain groups could either receive too many false credit approvals or too many denied credit applications due to historical data biases. By applying Equalized Odds, the model can be adjusted so that these rates are equalized between groups, resulting in fairer credit decisions.

However, the application of Equalized Odds also brings challenges. One of the biggest challenges is finding the right balance between fairness and accuracy. Fulfilling the Equalized Odds can reduce the overall accuracy of the model as additional constraints need to be considered. Furthermore, the implementation of this method can be complex, especially when the group characteristics are diverse and differently distributed.

Calibrated Equalized Odds

Calibrated Equalized Odds is an advanced method for improving the fairness and accuracy of machine learning models. This technique builds on the concept of equalized odds, but extends it to include the aspect of calibrating the predictions. The aim is both to equalize the error rates (false positive and false negative rates) between different demographic groups and to ensure the calibration of the probability predictions.

The concept of calibration in this context means that the predicted probabilities should match the actual probabilities. In other words, if a model predicts a 70% probability of a positive event, this event should actually occur 70% of the time. Calibration is important to ensure that the probabilities that the model outputs can be trusted and interpreted.

Calibrated Equalized Odds combines the goals of fairness through equalized odds with the requirement of calibration. This means that the method aims to ensure that the predicted probabilities are both equally calibrated between the groups and that the false-positive and false-negative rates are balanced.

To achieve calibrated equalized odds, a two-step process is typically used. In the first step, a prediction model is trained to maximize accuracy without regard to fairness. In the second step, a calibration layer is added that adjusts the predictions of the model to ensure equalized odds and calibration across the different groups.

A frequently used approach for calibration is isotonic regression or flat scaling. These methods adjust the probabilities to better match the actual results. In addition, an optimization routine can be used to ensure that the calibrated predictions satisfy the equalized odds condition. This can be achieved by introducing regularization terms into the loss function that minimize the deviations of the error rates and the calibration errors between the groups.

A practical example of the application of calibrated equalized odds is the development of a model for predicting recidivism rates among offenders. A standard model could have biases that lead to certain demographic groups being classified more frequently as high-risk. The use of calibrated equalized odds ensures that the error rates are the same for all groups and that the probability predictions are correctly calibrated. This enables fair and accurate predictions, leading to fairer decisions in the justice system.

The application of calibrated equalized odds brings with it a number of challenges. One of the biggest challenges is the complexity of implementation, as both calibrating the probabilities and ensuring fairness across groups must be achieved. This requires careful tuning of model parameters and possibly higher computational resources. Furthermore, the balance between fairness and accuracy can be difficult to achieve as additional constraints need to be included in the optimization.

Reject Option Classification

Reject Option Classification is a technique for improving fairness in machine learning models that aims to adjust or reject predictions in cases of high uncertainty, especially when these predictions could lead to unfair outcomes for certain demographic groups. This method recognizes and addresses situations where the model might make uncertain or potentially biased decisions and allows such decisions to be avoided or corrected.

The basic idea behind Reject Option Classification is that in cases of high uncertainty or potential bias, the model does not make a definitive decision, but instead rejects the prediction or applies an alternative decision method. This can be particularly important when the uncertainty of the model indicates that the decision is likely to be flawed or unfair to certain groups.

The process of implementing Reject Option Classification comprises several steps:

- Recognizing uncertainty: First, the model must be able to quantify uncertainty in its predictions. This can be done by calculating uncertainty measures such as the entropy of the prediction distribution, the variance of the probability predictions or other statistical uncertainty indicators. A high uncertainty indicates that the model is uncertain whether the prediction is correct.
- Definition of threshold values: Based on the uncertainty measures, threshold values are defined above which a prediction is rejected or adjusted. These thresholds can be calibrated so that they are particularly effective in cases where the prediction could lead to unfair results for certain groups.
- Reject or adjust the prediction: If the uncertainty exceeds a specified threshold, the model can reject the prediction and apply an alternative decision method instead. This could mean that the case is forwarded for further manual review or that a conservative decision is made that is less risky.

A practical example of the use of Reject Option Classification is the granting of credit. In cases where the model is unsure whether to approve or reject a loan application, it can reject the decision and forward the case for manual review. This is particularly important if the uncertainty indicates that the decision may be unfair to certain demographic groups due to bias or insufficient data.

There are several advantages to using this technique. By avoiding decisions in cases of high uncertainty, the likelihood of errors and unfair results is reduced. This helps to improve the overall fairness of the model and increase user confidence in the model's predictions. In addition, Reject Option Classification allows for targeted handling of difficult or sensitive cases, which can lead to better utilization of available resources.

However, there are also challenges when implementing Reject Option Classification. One of the biggest challenges is to set appropriate uncertainty thresholds. These thresholds need to be carefully calibrated to ensure that they are effective without affecting the performance of the model too much. Furthermore, the identification and quantification of uncertainty requires additional calculations and can increase the complexity of the model.

Continuous monitoring and audits

Correcting bias is not a one-off process, but requires continuous monitoring and regular audits of the models. This includes:

- Monitoring tools: Implement tools to continuously monitor model performance and fairness metrics during operation. These tools can trigger automatic alerts when distortions are detected.
- Regular audits: Systematic reviews of the models and their predictions by internal or external experts to ensure that the models continue to work

fairly and accurately. These audits should include both statistical analyses and qualitative assessments.
- Feedback loops: Setting up mechanisms that allow users to provide feedback on the AI's decisions. This feedback can be used to continuously improve the model and identify and rectify potential bias problems at an early stage.

Stakeholder involvement

The involvement of domain experts, ethicists and affected communities is also crucial to ensure that bias is addressed in a comprehensive and ethical manner. Through regular consultation and soliciting feedback, different perspectives and concerns can be taken into account, leading to more robust and equitable AI.

Identifying and correcting bias in AI systems is therefore a multi-layered and continuous process that requires various technical and organizational measures. By applying these techniques and creating a culture of fairness and transparency, developers and organizations can ensure that their AI models make fair and trustworthy decisions.

Tools and frameworks for bias analysis

There are a variety of tools and frameworks specifically designed to identify, analyze and minimize bias in artificial intelligence and machine learning models. These tools provide developers with the necessary tools to check their models for fairness and correct potential biases.

AI Fairness 360

AI Fairness 360 (AIF360) is a comprehensive open source toolkit developed by IBM to ensure fairness throughout the lifecycle of machine learning models. It provides a variety of metrics to analyze bias and several algorithms to mitigate bias in the pre-processing, in-processing and post-processing phases.

AIF360 includes various functions and features aimed at helping developers and data scientists identify and reduce bias in their models. Key features include various bias metrics, such as Disparate Impact and Equalized Odds. These metrics allow users to systematically assess the fairness of their models and identify specific areas where unfairness may exist.

In addition, AIF360 provides several algorithms designed to mitigate bias. These algorithms can be applied in different phases of model training and model development. In pre-processing, data can be transformed in such a way that existing biases are reduced. During in-processing, bias is addressed directly in the training process by adjusting algorithms to achieve fairer predictions. Finally, in post-processing, adjustments can be made to the results to ensure that the predictions remain fair, even if the underlying models exhibit bias.

Another important feature of AIF360 is the provision of interactive Jupyter notebooks and comprehensive tutorials. These resources make it easy for users to understand and integrate the various bias metrics and mitigation algorithms into their own machine learning workflows. The notebooks provide practical examples and step-by-step instructions that facilitate the implementation and use of the AIF360 tools.

Since AIF360 was developed in Python, it can be seamlessly integrated into existing machine learning workflows. This makes it a flexible and accessible tool for developers and data scientists interested in developing fair and ethical AI systems. The Python-based structure of AIF360 makes it possible to use the tools and algorithms at different stages of the modeling process, ensuring end-to-end fairness assurance.

In summary, AI Fairness 360 is a valuable toolkit for analyzing and mitigating bias in machine learning models. With its comprehensive metrics, algorithms and supporting resources, it provides developers and data scientists with the necessary tools to develop fair and equitable AI systems.

Fairness Indicators

Fairness Indicators is a tool developed by Google that helps developers create fair and responsible machine learning models. It provides a simple, scalable and flexible way to calculate and evaluate fairness metrics.

This tool enables the evaluation of fairness metrics across different demographic groups, which is particularly important to ensure that machine learning models do not have systematic biases against certain groups. Through systematic analysis and review, developers can ensure that their models make fair decisions, regardless of factors such as gender, age, ethnicity or other demographic characteristics.

A key feature of Fairness Indicators is the visualization tools that allow developers to create fairness dashboards. These dashboards provide an intuitive and easy-to-understand way to visualize and monitor the fairness of a model. By graphically representing the fairness metrics, developers and stakeholders can quickly and effectively identify where there may be inequities and where improvements are needed.

Fairness Indicators is specifically designed for integration into TensorFlow workflows. It seamlessly integrates with TensorFlow Extended (TFX), allowing developers to embed fairness assessments directly into their existing machine learning pipelines. This ensures continuous monitoring and improvement of fairness throughout the model development and deployment process.

Although Fairness Indicators is optimized for integration with TensorFlow, it also supports other frameworks. This gives developers the flexibility to use the tool in different machine learning environments, regardless of the specific technology they prefer. This interoperability ensures that Fairness Indicators has broad application and can contribute to improving fairness in different contexts.

In summary, Google's Fairness Indicators provides a valuable resource for developers looking to create fair and responsible machine learning models. With its powerful tools for calculating and visualizing fairness metrics and seamless integration with TensorFlow workflows, it ensures that developers can systematically evaluate and improve the fairness of their models. These features make Fairness Indicators an indispensable tool in the development of ethical AI systems.

Fairlearn

Fairlearn is an open source project from Microsoft that helps developers identify and fix fairness issues in their machine learning models. This toolset provides comprehensive resources for assessing and mitigating bias, making it an important tool for developing fair and ethical AI systems.

A key feature of Fairlearn is its fairness metrics and bias mitigation algorithms. These metrics allow developers to systematically evaluate the fairness of their models by analyzing different demographic groups and highlighting how different groups may be treated differently. The bias mitigation algorithms provide specific techniques to reduce or eliminate identified biases. These algorithms can be applied to different stages of model training to ensure that the resulting models are fair and equitable.

Another important feature of Fairlearn is the visualization tools used to illustrate fairness issues. These visualizations allow developers to present the results of their fairness analyses in an intuitive and easy-to-understand way. By graphically representing fairness metrics and bias mitigation measures, developers and stakeholders can quickly see where inequities exist and how effective the corrective actions applied are. This visual transparency is critical to building confidence in the fairness of models and making informed decisions about their use.

Fairlearn is compatible with common machine learning frameworks such as scikit-learn, which facilitates its integration into existing workflows. This compatibility ensures that developers can easily incorporate the toolset into their existing machine learning pipelines. The seamless integration makes it possible to embed fairness analysis and bias mitigation strategies directly into the development process, ensuring continuous improvements in model fairness.

Since Fairlearn is Python-based, it can be flexibly integrated into various machine learning workflows. This flexibility makes it a versatile tool that can be used in different contexts and application areas. Developers can use Fairlearn to create new models as well as review and improve existing models, leading to a broad application of the toolset.

Overall, Microsoft's Fairlearn provides a comprehensive solution for detecting and fixing fairness issues in machine learning models. With its powerful fairness metrics, bias mitigation algorithms and vivid visualization tools, it ensures that developers are able to build fair and responsible AI systems. These features make Fairlearn an indispensable tool in modern machine learning development.

What-If Tool

Google's What-If Tool is a powerful tool that allows developers to explore their models in depth and run different scenarios to analyze the impact on fairness. It aims to increase the transparency and comprehensibility of machine learning models by providing interactive and user-friendly visualizations.

One of the main features of the What-If tool are the interactive visualizations for model evaluation. These visualizations allow developers to intuitively understand how their models work and how they react to different input data. By graphically representing model results, complex relationships and potential fairness issues can be more easily identified and analyzed. These visualizations are particularly useful for comparing model performance across different demographic groups and uncovering systematic inequities.

Another key feature of the What-If tool is the ability to run "what-if" scenarios. Developers can make hypothetical changes to the input data and observe how these changes affect the model predictions. This feature is extremely valuable in understanding how robust and fair a model is when certain parameters change. It provides an in-depth insight into the sensitivity of the model and allows potential weaknesses and sources of bias to be identified and addressed.

The What-If tool supports models developed with TensorFlow and AI Platform, which seamlessly integrates it into existing Google ecosystems. This support makes it easy to integrate the tool into existing machine learning projects and implement model evaluation into the development process. Developers can analyze their TensorFlow models directly in the What-If tool and visualize the results in real time.

Another benefit of the What-If tool is its ability to integrate with Jupyter Notebooks and other development environments. This allows developers to incorporate the tool into their preferred working environments and seamlessly integrate model evaluation and analysis into their existing workflows. The flexibility and ease of use of the tool make it a valuable addition to any machine learning development environment.

Overall, Google's What-If tool offers a comprehensive solution for investigating and analyzing machine learning models with a special focus on fairness. The interactive visualizations and the ability to play through "what-if" scenarios provide deep insights into the functioning and fairness of models. The support for TensorFlow and AI Platform as well as the integration capability in Jupyter Notebooks and other development environments make it an indispensable tool for developers who want to develop fair and transparent AI systems.

Themis-ML

Themis-ML is an open-source toolkit that aims to detect and reduce bias in machine learning models. This toolkit provides a comprehensive collection of tools specifically designed to analyze and mitigate bias. Themis-ML is aimed at developers and data scientists who want to create fair and ethical machine learning models.

A key feature of Themis-ML is its support for various bias metrics and mitigation techniques. These bias metrics allow users to systematically evaluate the fairness of their models by analyzing different demographic groups and identifying inequalities in model predictions. By applying these metrics, developers can specifically identify areas where their models may be discriminatory.

In addition to bias metrics, Themis-ML also offers a range of bias mitigation techniques. These techniques can be used at different stages of the machine learning process to ensure that the resulting models are fair and equitable. The mitigation techniques range from adjustments to the data before model training (pre-processing) to modifications during the training process (in-processing) and post-processing of the model results. By applying these techniques, developers can reduce or eliminate systematic distortions in their models.

Themis-ML is compatible with the widely used machine learning framework scikit-learn. This compatibility ensures that developers can easily integrate Themis-ML into their existing scikit-learn workflows. The seamless integration makes it possible to incorporate bias analysis and mitigation directly into the development process without the need for extensive customization or additional resources.

Since Themis-ML is Python-based, it can be flexibly and easily integrated into various machine learning environments. This flexibility makes it a versatile tool that can be used in different contexts and application areas. Developers can use Themis-ML to create new models as well as to review and improve existing models, ensuring a broad application of the toolset.

Overall, Themis-ML provides a comprehensive solution for detecting and mitigating bias in machine learning models. With its support for various bias metrics and mitigation techniques, as well as compatibility with scikit-learn, it ensures that developers are able to build fair and responsible AI systems. Its Python-based structure and easy integration into existing workflows make Themis-ML an indispensable tool in modern machine learning development.

LIME (Local Interpretable Model-agnostic Explanations)

LIME (Local Interpretable Model-agnostic Explanations) is a model interpretation tool that helps developers to better understand the decision-making processes of their machine learning models. It provides an in-depth analysis of model decisions by showing which features influence the decisions. This can also help to identify and analyze bias.

A key feature of LIME is its ability to explain model decisions using locally interpretable models. LIME works by approximating the predictions of a complex model locally by simpler, interpretable models. These local models provide an understandable representation that allows developers to see which features in a particular context (i.e. near a particular data point) influence the model prediction the most. This local interpretation allows developers to understand how the model works in specific cases, increasing transparency and confidence in model predictions.

Another advantage of LIME is its support for different types of models and data. It is model-agnostic, which means that it is compatible with a variety of model types, including decision trees, neural networks and support vector machines. LIME can also work with different types of data, be it structured data, text data or image data. This versatility makes LIME an extremely useful tool in various machine learning applications.

LIME is Python-based and has become widely used in the machine learning community. The Python implementation facilitates integration into existing machine learning workflows and enables ease of use and application. Developers can incorporate LIME into their analyses to check the decision logic of their models and identify potential bias. The comprehensive documentation and numerous examples from the community help users to use LIME effectively and benefit from the experience of others.

In summary, LIME provides a valuable method for interpreting model decisions and detecting bias. The ability to explain complex model predictions through locally interpretable models allows developers to gain a deeper understanding of how their models work. The support for different model types and data sets, as well as its widespread use in the Python-based machine learning community, make LIME an indispensable tool for developing transparent and fair AI systems.

SHAP (SHapley Additive exPlanations)

SHAP (SHapley Additive exPlanations) is an advanced model interpretation tool based on Shapley values. It supports developers in understanding the contributions of individual features to the model decision. SHAP uses concepts from game theory to ensure fair and consistent attribution of feature influences on model predictions.

A central feature of SHAP is the calculation of Shapley values to explain model predictions. Shapley values provide a mathematically sound method to quantify the influence of each feature on the prediction of a model. These values are particularly useful as they not only represent the contribution of each feature to the prediction, but also ensure that the sum of the Shapley values of all features correctly reflects the difference between the prediction and the average value of the predictions. This allows for a fair distribution of influencing factors and helps developers understand how and why a model makes certain decisions.

In addition, SHAP offers powerful visualization tools that facilitate the interpretation of the results. The visualizations include Summary Plots, Dependence Plots, Force Plots and Interaction Plots. These graphical representations help to intuitively grasp the influences of the features on the model predictions and to recognize complex relationships between the features and the model decisions. The force plots in particular offer a detailed view that shows how the individual features add up to a specific prediction.

SHAP is Python-based and compatible with many popular machine learning frameworks such as scikit-learn, XGBoost, LightGBM, Keras, and TensorFlow. This compatibility facilitates the integration of SHAP into existing machine learning workflows and enables developers to seamlessly integrate model interpretation into their development process. The comprehensive support of various frameworks makes SHAP a versatile and flexible tool that can be used in a variety of application scenarios.

In summary, SHAP provides a precise and consistent method for model interpretation through the calculation of Shapley values. SHAP's visualization tools help developers to interpret the results of these calculations in an understandable and intuitive way. Due to its Python-based structure and broad compatibility with various machine learning frameworks, SHAP is an indispensable tool for creating transparent and comprehensible machine learning models. Using SHAP helps developers better understand the decision making of their models and ensure that their models are fair and accountable.

DEon (Datasheets for Datasets)

DEon is a tool developed by the Partnership on AI to help developers create systematic documentation for their datasets. These so-called "datasheets" provide a structured method for capturing and presenting important information about datasets, which is a crucial step in identifying and avoiding bias.

A key feature of DEon is the provision of templates and guidelines for the creation of datasheets. These templates help developers to document all relevant aspects of a dataset, including the origin of the data, the methods used to process the data and any known biases. By systematically documenting this information, developers can gain a deeper understanding of their datasets and identify and address potential sources of bias at an early stage.

DEon supports the documentation of data set origin, processing methods and known biases. This is particularly important as it creates transparency and enables detailed traceability. By accurately recording the origin and processing of the data, developers can better understand how and why certain biases have arisen and take targeted action to mitigate these biases.

The DEon application can be seamlessly integrated into the data management process. This enables developers to establish the creation and maintenance of datasheets as an integral part of their workflow, ensuring continuous monitoring and documentation of data sets.

The effective use of tools and frameworks to ensure fairness and transparency in machine learning models requires integration into existing machine learning workflows. A typical process could look like this:

- Data preparation: Before modeling, the data set is checked for bias using tools such as AIF360 or Fairlearn. Pre-processing techniques are used to clean and adjust the data to minimize bias. DEon is used to create comprehensive datasheets that document the origin, processing and known biases of the data.
- Model training: During training, in-processing techniques are used to reduce bias. This could include the implementation of fairness constraints or the use of adversarial networks aimed at developing fair and balanced models.
- Model evaluation: After training, the model is evaluated using tools such as the What-If Tool (WIT), Fairness Indicators or SHAP to ensure that it is fair and unbiased. These tools provide detailed insights into the model decisions and help to identify and address potential sources of bias.

- Regular monitoring: Once the model is deployed, performance is continuously monitored and regularly reviewed using the above tools to ensure that no new biases occur. This regular monitoring is crucial to ensure that the model remains fair even under changing conditions.

By integrating these tools and frameworks into the overall machine learning process, developers can ensure that their models are fair, transparent and responsible. The systematic application of these methods helps to build trust in AI systems and raise ethical standards in machine learning development.

By applying these tools and techniques, developers can ensure that their AI systems are fair, transparent and trustworthy. This is crucial to gaining the trust of users and promoting the long-term acceptance of AI technologies in society.

Transparency in algorithms and models

Transparency in algorithms and models is a decisive factor in promoting trust in artificial intelligence and machine learning. Transparency means that the functioning of algorithms and the decision-making processes of models are comprehensible and understandable for developers, users and those affected. This requires a combination of technical measures, best practices and organizational strategies. Here are some techniques for promoting transparency in algorithms and models.

Explainable AI (XAI)

Explainable AI aims to make the decision-making processes of AI models understandable. This includes the development of models and algorithms that can explain their decisions in a way that is comprehensible to humans. Methods for explainable AI are:

The explanation of models in machine learning is of crucial importance in order to increase the trust and acceptance of these technologies in various applications. In the following, the methods LIME, SHAP as well as model-internal methods and model maps are described and compared in more detail.

LIME (Local Interpretable Model-agnostic Explanations)

LIME is a technique that aims to make the predictions of arbitrary models understandable by creating local, interpretable models that mimic the decisions of a complex model near a particular data point. LIME works by generating slightly altered data sets and observing the effects of these changes on the model's predictions. By fitting a simple, interpreted model, such as a linear regression, to these modified datasets, LIME can show how each feature contributes to the prediction. This provides a detailed insight into the model's decision-making processes at a local level.

SHAP (SHapley Additive exPlanations)

SHAP values are based on principles of game theory and provide a consistent method for assigning influence values for each feature on the model prediction. SHAP values quantify how much each feature contributes to the difference between the actual prediction and a baseline prediction by analyzing the effects of all possible combinations of features. This additive property of SHAP enables a comprehensive and transparent explanation of model predictions as it clearly shows the contribution of each feature to the overall output of the model.

Internal model methods

Transparent models

Simple models such as decision trees, linear regression models and rule-based systems are inherently more understandable and transparent than complex models such as deep neural networks. These intrinsically transparent models provide a clear and intuitive interpretation of the relationships between the input data and the predictions. Decision trees, for example, visualize the decision paths that the model takes to arrive at a particular prediction, allowing for an easy-to-understand explanation of the model logic.

Attention Mechanisms

In neural networks, especially in sequential models such as RNNs or transformers, attention mechanisms can be used to emphasize the relevant parts of the input data that contribute to the prediction. These mechanisms weight different parts of the input sequence based on their relevance to the current prediction. This makes it possible to visualize the focus of the model on specific data points and understand which parts of the input contribute most to the output.

Documentation and communication

Model Cards, developed by Google AI, provide standardized documentation for ML models. They contain comprehensive information about a model's development, scope, performance metrics and known limitations. This documentation aims to promote transparency and help users understand the strengths and weaknesses of a model. By providing structured and detailed information, model cards support responsible use and confidence in ML models by providing clarity on their functionality and application limitations.

The selection of the appropriate method for explaining ML models depends heavily on the use case and the specific requirements. LIME and SHAP offer flexible, model-independent approaches to make the predictions of complex models understandable. Model-internal methods such as transparent models and attention mechanisms, on the other hand, offer natural comprehensibility and traceability. Model maps complement these technical approaches with comprehensive documentation and thus promote transparency and trust in ML models.

Each of these methods has its own strengths and, depending on the context and requirements, is differently suited to improving the explainability of models and thus increasing their acceptance and trustworthiness.

Datasheets for datasets

Transparency in algorithms and models is essential to strengthen trust in AI systems. The use of explainable AI methods, comprehensive documentation, the use of fairness tools, technical measures and organizational strategies are crucial to ensure that AI models are transparent, fair and responsible. These measures help to promote acceptance and trust in AI technologies and fully exploit their potential for the benefit of society.

Datasheets for datasets, developed by the Partnership on AI, are used for the systematic documentation of datasets. They contain information about the origin of the data, the collection methods, the processing steps and the known biases. This transparency in the data sources is crucial for the evaluation of model quality.

AI Fairness 360 (AIF360) provides a variety of bias analysis metrics and bias mitigation algorithms. By using these tools, developers can ensure that their models are fair and unbiased. The results of these analyses should be documented and communicated transparently. Fairlearn, developed by Microsoft, also offers tools for assessing and mitigating bias in machine learning models. It enables the analysis and visualization of fairness metrics, which contributes to the transparency of model decisions.

Audit trails record all decisions and processes that take place during the development and operation of an AI model. These records can be used to understand how and why certain decisions were made, which contributes to transparency and accountability. Developers should also disclose the model architecture and the hyperparameters used. This allows others to better understand the structure and functionality of the model. By publishing the source code and algorithms, developers can increase the transparency of their models. Open source projects allow the community to review, validate and improve the algorithms.

Interdisciplinary teams that combine expertise from different areas such as data science, ethics, law and domain knowledge can provide a broader perspective on the development and use of AI models. This diversity promotes transparency and understanding of the models. Organizations should provide regular training and awareness programs to educate employees on the importance of transparency, fairness and accountability in AI systems. Companies should develop and implement ethical policies and compliance programs that promote the principles of transparency and fairness in AI development and use. This includes the establishment of ethics committees to monitor compliance with these guidelines.

Transparency in algorithms and models can be achieved by combining these different approaches and measures. Developers and organizations must continuously strive to improve their practices and embed the principles of transparency and fairness in their processes. Only through these comprehensive efforts can the full potential of AI technologies be exploited responsibly and for the benefit of society.

The importance of transparency for trust

Transparency in the development and use of artificial intelligence is of fundamental importance for trust in these technologies. Trust in AI systems does not arise by itself; it must be built through careful and deliberate measures that ensure that the processes, algorithms and decision-making mechanisms of AI are clear and comprehensible to all stakeholders. Transparency plays a crucial role in this by creating the basis for trust and acceptance.

When users, developers and the general public do not understand how AI systems work, a natural skepticism arises. This skepticism is often the result of uncertainty and ignorance about how AI models make decisions. Without a clear understanding of the underlying mechanisms and logic, there remains a certain unpredictability that undermines trust. Transparency helps to close this gap by providing insights into the inner workings of AI. When the processes are open and the decisions are explainable, users feel safer and have more trust in the technology.

A key aspect of transparency is the explainability of AI decisions. Explainable AI (XAI) aims to make the decision-making process of models understandable. This means that the models not only deliver results, but also make it clear why and how these results were achieved. If users understand the reasons behind a decision, they can better assess the correctness and appropriateness of that decision. This is particularly important in sensitive areas such as healthcare, justice or finance, where the impact of AI decisions can directly affect people's lives and well-being.

Transparency also promotes accountability. When the processes and decisions of AI systems are open, developers and operators can be held accountable. This creates a mechanism for review and scrutiny that ensures systems are operated according to ethical and legal standards. The ability to review and audit AI decisions by independent parties strengthens confidence in the integrity and fairness of the systems. Without this possibility, wrong decisions and bias could remain undetected, which would significantly impair trust.

The disclosure of model architectures, algorithms and data sets is another important component of transparency. When developers disclose their models and the data sources used, they enable comprehensive review and evaluation by the scientific community and other stakeholders. This not only promotes trust, but also contributes to the continuous improvement and further development of the technology. Open models and data allow others to identify errors and weaknesses and make suggestions for optimization. This collaborative approach strengthens the robustness and reliability of AI systems.

Transparency also plays a crucial role in the perception of fairness. If users and stakeholders understand how decisions are made and what data is used, they can better assess whether the processes are fair and unbiased. This is particularly relevant in contexts where historical bias and discrimination may be present in the data. By disclosing the data processing and decision-making processes, developers can ensure that their systems are fair and inclusive. Transparency also makes it possible to identify and address biases early on, before they influence model decisions.

Another aspect of transparency is the clear communication and documentation of the limitations and uncertainties of AI systems. No model is perfect, and it is important that the limitations and uncertainties of the technology are openly communicated. When users know the areas where AI may be inaccurate or uncertain, they can make more informed decisions about how to use and interpret the results. This honest communication goes a long way to preventing unrealistic expectations and increasing trust in the technology.

Finally, transparency also contributes to the ethical acceptance of AI. In a world where ethical considerations are becoming increasingly important, being transparent about the ethical foundations and principles by which AI systems are developed and operated is crucial. This includes disclosing ethical guidelines, complying with data protection regulations and ensuring that systems promote the well-being of users and society as a whole. Transparency in these areas shows that developers and operators are taking responsibility and taking the impact of their technology on society seriously.

Implementation of security protocols

The implementation of security protocols in Artificial Intelligence (AI) systems is essential to ensure their integrity, confidentiality and availability. Security protocols protect AI systems from a variety of threats, including cyberattacks, data tampering and unauthorized access. The following aspects and strategies provide a comprehensive approach to implementing effective security protocols.

Data security and data protection

Encrypting data, both at rest and in transit, is a fundamental security measure. This prevents unauthorized access and protects sensitive information from theft and misuse. Symmetric and asymmetric encryption methods, such as AES and RSA, provide robust protection mechanisms. Strict access control ensures that only authorized users can access the data and the AI system. This includes the implementation of multi-factor authentication (MFA), role-based access control (RBAC) and fine-grained permissions. MFA increases security by requiring additional authentication factors such as biometrics or one-time passwords.

Model and system integrity

Regular security audits and penetration tests are critical to identifying and remediating vulnerabilities in AI systems. These tests should be conducted by independent security experts to ensure that potential attack vectors are identified and mitigated. Version control systems (such as Git) and detailed audit trails help to track changes to the models and system architecture. This facilitates the identification of changes and potential vulnerabilities introduced by software updates or model adaptations.

Protection against adversarial attacks

AI models should be tested against adversarial attacks where malicious inputs are used to manipulate the model. Techniques such as adversarial training, where the model is trained with intentionally perturbed data, can increase robustness against such attacks. Anomaly detection systems can identify unusual activity or input that could indicate an attack. By monitoring input data streams and model predictions, suspicious patterns can be detected early and appropriate action taken.

Safe development practices

The integration of security considerations into the entire development cycle is crucial. The Secure Software Development Life Cycle (SDLC) encompasses the planning, development, testing, deployment and maintenance of AI systems with security requirements in mind. Security testing and threat modeling should be performed at every stage of the SDLC. Regular code reviews and static code analyses help to identify security gaps and vulnerabilities in the source code. Automated tools such as SonarQube or Checkmarx can assist in the detection of security issues.

Data protection and compliance

Compliance with data protection laws and guidelines such as the General Data Protection Regulation (GDPR) in the EU or the California Consumer Privacy Act (CCPA) is essential. This includes the implementation of data protection measures such as data minimization, purpose limitation and data subject rights. Techniques for anonymizing and pseudonymizing personal data protect the privacy of users. This reduces the risk of sensitive information being compromised if a data leak occurs.

Ongoing monitoring and incident response

Continuous monitoring of systems for security incidents is essential. Security Information and Event

Management (SIEM) systems aggregate and analyze security events in real time to quickly identify threats. A clearly defined incident response plan ensures that the team is prepared for security incidents. This plan should include processes for detecting, assessing, containing and resolving security incidents and communicating with stakeholders.

Training and sensitization

Regular training and awareness programs for employees promote awareness of security risks and best practices. Training should focus on topics such as phishing, secure password practices and security incident detection. Promoting a culture of security within the organization is critical. Employees should be encouraged to report potential security issues and actively contribute to the security of systems.

Implementing security protocols in AI systems is a multi-layered and continuous process that includes technological measures, best practices and organizational strategies. By ensuring data security, model integrity, protection against adversarial attacks, adherence to secure development practices, data protection and ongoing monitoring, developers and organizations can create robust and trustworthy AI systems. These measures help to increase trust in AI technologies and promote their safe and responsible use.

Future prospects

Current developments in AI research on error prevention

The future prospects of artificial intelligence are closely linked to continuous progress in research and development, particularly in the area of error prevention and improving the reliability and fairness of AI systems. The following developments and trends show how AI research aims to minimize errors and increase the performance and trustworthiness of AI technologies.

Improving explainability and transparency

A central focus of future AI research is on improving the explainability and transparency of AI models. Explainable AI (XAI) is becoming increasingly important in order to overcome the "black box" nature of many AI systems. New approaches and technologies aim to make the decision-making processes of AI models more understandable. This includes developing methods for visualizing decision paths, providing detailed explanations for individual predictions and implementing models that are intrinsically understandable.

Integration of ethical and legal aspects

Compliance with ethical and legal standards is becoming increasingly important in AI research. Future developments aim to design AI systems in such a way that they not only meet technical requirements, but also take ethical considerations into account. This includes integrating fairness metrics, ensuring data protection and taking ethical guidelines into account when developing and implementing AI systems. Research focuses on developing algorithms that do not discriminate and respect the rights and privacy of users.

Advances in robustness and safety

The robustness of AI systems against adversarial attacks and unforeseen inputs is another important area of research. New techniques in the area of adversarial training and security checks are being developed to make models more resistant to manipulation and attacks. The continuous monitoring and adaptation of models and the implementation of anomaly detection mechanisms help to increase the security and reliability of AI systems.

Development of hybrid models

Hybrid models that combine different AI techniques are a promising approach to error prevention. These models use the strengths of different methods to compensate for the weaknesses of individual approaches. For example, hybrid models can combine neural networks with rule-based systems or statistical methods to achieve more robust and accurate predictions. Research in this area aims to integrate the best features of different techniques and develop models that are more versatile and reliable.

Automated machine learning (AutoML)

AutoML techniques automate many of the steps in the machine learning process, including model selection, hyperparameter optimization and feature engineering. These technologies help to minimize human error and increase the efficiency of model development. Future developments in AutoML will aim to further optimize the entire machine learning workflow and lower the barriers to the use of AI. By automating complex processes, more accurate and robust models can be created faster and with less effort.

Use of federated learning

Federated learning is an approach that makes it possible to train AI models on distributed data sources without having to centralize the data. This improves data privacy and security as sensitive data does not need to be transferred or shared. Federated learning also helps to increase the generalizability of models by enabling training on diverse and decentralized data sets. Future developments in this area will aim to improve the efficiency and scalability of federated learning and enable new applications.

Improved bias detection and fairness algorithms

The detection and correction of bias in AI models remains a key area of research. New algorithms and techniques for bias detection and mitigation are being developed to ensure that AI systems are fair and unbiased. These techniques include pre-processing methods to clean the training data as well as in-processing and post-processing methods to adjust the models and their predictions. The continuous development of these technologies will help to ensure the fairness and equity of AI systems.

Use of quantum computing

Quantum computing has the potential to significantly increase the performance of AI systems. Quantum computers can solve complex calculations and optimization problems much faster than conventional computers. Research in the field of quantum machine learning is investigating how quantum algorithms can be used to improve training processes and solve previously unsolvable problems. Future developments in this area could lead to significant advances in the efficiency and accuracy of AI models.

Expansion of interdisciplinary cooperation

Future AI research will be increasingly interdisciplinary and involve experts from different fields such as computer science, ethics, law, sociology and economics. This collaboration will make it possible to develop more comprehensive and holistic approaches to the development and implementation of AI systems. Interdisciplinary teams can bring different perspectives and expertise to ensure that AI technologies are used responsibly and for the benefit of society.

The future of AI research into error prevention is characterized by a variety of exciting developments and approaches. From improving explainability and transparency to integrating ethical and legal aspects and increasing robustness and safety, the continuous development of AI technologies aims to ensure the reliability, fairness and trustworthiness of AI systems. By using new techniques such as hybrid models, AutoML, federated learning and quantum computing, and by promoting interdisciplinary collaboration, AI research will continue to develop innovative solutions to prevent errors and improve performance. These advances will be instrumental in realizing the full potential of AI technologies and promoting their sustainable and responsible use in society.

New approaches in data processing and modeling

The rapid development of artificial intelligence and machine learning has led to a variety of new approaches in data processing and modeling. These new methods aim to improve the efficiency, accuracy and robustness of AI systems. Here are some of the most innovative approaches currently being developed and used in research and practice.

Transfer Learning

Transfer learning is an approach in which a model that has already been pre-trained on a large amount of data is transferred to a specific, often smaller task. This makes it possible to train models faster and more effectively with less data, as the model has already learned basic features and structures. Transfer learning is particularly useful in areas where labeled data is scarce, such as medical image processing.

Self-monitored learning

Self-supervised learning is an emerging approach in which models learn from unlabeled data by supervising themselves over the data context. This can be achieved through tasks such as predicting missing parts of an image or the next word in a text. Self-supervised learning reduces the dependency on large labeled datasets and enables the use of the vast amounts of unlabeled data that are available.

Few-Shot Learning

Few-shot learning aims to develop models that can learn from just a few examples. This is particularly useful in scenarios where only a few labeled data points are available. Techniques such as meta-learning, where the model learns as you learn, are central to this approach. Few-shot learning makes it possible to quickly adapt and deploy AI systems in new domains.

Generative models

Generative models such as Generative Adversarial Networks (GANs) and Variational Autoencoders (VAEs) are able to generate new data points that are similar to the training data. These models are used in various applications, from image generation to data synthesis, and help to improve data availability and data quality. They are particularly useful in data augmentation and training models in data-poor environments.

Graph Neural Networks (GNNs)

Graph Neural Networks are specialized models designed to work on data that can be represented as graphs. This is particularly useful for data with complex relationships, such as social networks, molecular structures or transportation networks. GNNs can directly model the topology of the data and thus make more accurate and intuitive predictions.

Reinforcement Learning (RL)

Reinforcement learning, especially deep reinforcement learning, has achieved remarkable success in areas such as games, robotics and autonomous driving. RL models learn by interacting with their environment and receive rewards or penalties for certain actions. This method is particularly effective for problems involving sequential decisions and long-term optimization.

Explainable AI (XAI)

Explainable AI aims to make the decision-making processes of AI models more comprehensible. New approaches in explainable AI include techniques such as SHAP (SHapley Additive exPlanations) and LIME (Local Interpretable Model-agnostic Explanations), which help to explain the contributions of individual features to the predictions of a model. XAI is particularly important for applications in regulated areas where transparency and traceability are crucial.

Bayesian methods

Bayesian methods integrate uncertainties into the model predictions, which leads to more robust and reliable results. These methods are particularly useful in areas where uncertainty and variability play a major role, such as in medicine or financial forecasting. Bayesian networks and Gaussian processes are examples of such approaches.

Edge AI

Edge AI refers to the execution of AI models directly on devices at the edge of the network, such as smartphones, IoT devices and sensors. This reduces latency and the need for data transfer to central servers, increasing efficiency and security. New developments in model compression and optimized hardware acceleration make Edge AI increasingly practical and powerful.

Multimodal models

Multimodal models combine data from different sources, such as text, images and audio, to make more comprehensive and accurate predictions. These models are particularly useful for complex applications such as autonomous vehicles that rely on visual, auditory and other sensory data simultaneously. The integration of different data modalities makes it possible to develop richer and more context-aware models.

Continuous Learning

Continuous learning (or lifelong learning) is an approach in which AI models continuously learn from new data without forgetting what they have already learned. This is particularly important for applications that are constantly evolving, such as personalized recommendations or adaptive learning. Continuous learning techniques help to solve the problem of "catastrophic forgetting", where a model learns new information but loses old information in the process.

The new approaches in data processing and modeling are driving the next generation of AI systems by improving efficiency, accuracy and robustness. These innovations help overcome the challenges associated with scaling and applying AI in real-world scenarios. By integrating these advanced methods, developers and researchers can ensure that AI systems become more reliable, fair and adaptable, ultimately leading to wider acceptance and use of AI technologies in society.

Research initiatives and projects

Research initiatives and projects in the field of artificial intelligence play a crucial role in fostering innovation and tackling complex challenges. These initiatives range from academic research programs to industry consortia and international collaborations and focus on various aspects of AI, including machine learning, ethics, explainability and robustness.

OpenAI is a leading research organization focused on the development and advancement of secure and general artificial intelligence (AGI). A well-known project of OpenAI is GPT (Generative Pre-trained Transformer), which is known for its advances in the field of natural language processing. OpenAI is also heavily involved in research on the safety and ethics of AI and regularly publishes research results and tools that are accessible to the wider community.

Google AI is the research division of Google that focuses on advanced AI and machine learning. Significant projects include TensorFlow, an open source software library for machine learning, and the development of algorithms for self-driving cars, medical diagnostics and language processing. Google AI also promotes the explainability and fairness of AI through initiatives such as the What-If Tool and Model Cards.

DeepMind, a subsidiary of Alphabet, is known for its pioneering work in the application of deep learning and reinforcement learning. One notable project is AlphaGo, which defeated a human Go master for the first time. DeepMind also conducts intensive research into applications in medicine, such as the use of AI to predict kidney disease and analyze eye diseases.

The Partnership on AI is a non-profit organization founded by leading technology companies such as Amazon, Apple, Facebook, Google and Microsoft. It aims to promote research and dialog on the ethical, social and economic impact of AI. The organization supports projects and working groups that deal with topics such as fairness, transparency, explainability and data protection in AI.

AI4EU is a European project funded by the European Commission to create a common platform for AI in Europe. The project aims to support research and innovation in AI and provide a wide range of services, tools and data for researchers, companies and policy makers. AI4EU also promotes collaboration between different actors in the AI ecosystem.

FAIR is Facebook's research department that focuses on the development of AI technologies. Projects include advances in computer vision, natural language processing and machine learning. FAIR regularly publishes research papers and open source tools to support the AI community. One notable project is PyTorch, an open source machine learning library that is widely used.

IBM Research AI is the AI research division of IBM and has made significant contributions to the development of AI technologies. Watson, IBM's cognitive computing system, is a well-known example that is used in various fields such as healthcare, financial services and education. IBM Research AI also focuses on the explainability, fairness and safety of AI systems.

The MIT-IBM Watson AI Lab is a joint research initiative of the Massachusetts Institute of Technology (MIT) and IBM. The lab conducts research on a variety of topics, including fundamental advances in AI, the application of AI in industry, and exploring the societal impact of AI. The collaboration aims to push the boundaries of AI and develop innovative solutions to real-world problems.

Stanford University's Human-Centered AI Initiative promotes the research and development of AI systems that are human-centered and ethically responsible. The initiative explores the social and ethical implications of AI and develops technologies that promote human well-being. HAI promotes interdisciplinary research and collaboration to maximize the positive impact of AI on society.

The Alan Turing Institute is the UK's national institute for data science and AI. It promotes cutting-edge research in machine learning, data science and AI. The Institute works closely with industry partners and public institutions to develop innovative solutions and promote the application of AI across different sectors.

OpenAI has made significant progress in multimodal AI research with the DALL-E and CLIP projects. DALL-E is a model that can generate realistic images from text descriptions, while CLIP (Contrastive Language-Image Pretraining) aims to link images and text in a way that enables powerful visual search and interpretation. These projects demonstrate the potential of AI to go beyond individual modalities and tackle complex tasks.

Initiative for the Integration of AI into Society (I-AIM) is a global initiative that focuses on the integration of AI into society. It promotes the research and development of AI technologies that address social and economic challenges. The initiative works on projects that aim to improve healthcare, education and public administration by implementing and disseminating AI solutions.

Conclusion

Ultimately, it's about what grows faster: the opportunities or the risks of artificial intelligence

On the one hand, AI offers numerous advantages and potential in many areas. In medicine, AI supports the diagnosis and treatment of diseases, personalized medicine and the development of new drugs. Through advanced imaging techniques and data analysis, AI leads to more accurate diagnoses and more efficient treatment plans. AI is also helping to increase productivity and efficiency in business by automating and optimizing processes. By taking over repeatable tasks, human workers can focus on more creative and complex work. AI also helps to solve environmental problems by recognizing patterns in large amounts of data and thus using resources more efficiently and reducing emissions. In education and research, AI expands access to knowledge and accelerates scientific discoveries. Everyday applications such as personalized recommendations, voice assistants and autonomous vehicles improve convenience and efficiency in daily life.

At the same time, there are considerable risks and challenges associated with the use of AI. One major problem is the reinforcement of existing prejudices and discrimination when AI systems are trained on biased data. This can lead to unfair decisions in areas such as criminal justice, lending and employment. Automation through AI can also lead to significant job losses, especially in industries that rely heavily on routine tasks. This requires comprehensive strategies to retrain and upskill the affected workforce. Security risks from tampering and cyber-attacks pose a further threat, as malicious actors could use AI to cause harm, whether through targeted attacks, disinformation or other criminal activity. Many AI systems, especially those based on deep learning, are "black boxes" whose decision-making processes are difficult to understand. This makes the traceability and accountability of AI decisions more difficult. The development and use of AI also raises complex ethical issues, including responsibility for decisions made by AI systems and the long-term impact on society.

The opportunities of AI are growing in parallel with the risks, and it is difficult to make a general statement about whether the risks are growing faster than the opportunities. A key point is that the speed of growth of risks and opportunities depends heavily on regulation, the implementation of ethical guidelines and social acceptance. Through careful and thoughtful development and the use of security and ethics protocols, many risks can be mitigated. However, this requires a proactive approach from politics, business and science. Investment in research to identify and mitigate bias, improve the transparency of AI systems and develop robust safety measures is essential.

It cannot be said unequivocally that the risks of AI are growing faster than the opportunities. Both are developing rapidly and in parallel. What is important is that society takes both the opportunities and the risks seriously and takes targeted measures to maximize the benefits of AI while minimizing the risks. Through responsible innovation, comprehensive regulation and ethical considerations, a balance can be found that harnesses the benefits of AI and mitigates its potential dangers.